OPPOSING VIEWPOINTS® SERIES

Obesity

Other Books of Related Interest:

Opposing Viewpoints Series

Health

At Issue Series

Fast Food

Current Controversies Series

Health Care

"Congress shall make no law . . . abridging the freedom of speech, or of the press."

First Amendment to the U.S. Constitution

The basic foundation of our democracy is the First Amendment guarantee of freedom of expression. The Opposing Viewpoints Series is dedicated to the concept of this basic freedom and the idea that it is more important to practice it than to enshrine it.

OPPOSING
VIEWPOINTS®
SERIES

Obesity

Scott Barbour, book editor

GREENHAVEN PRESS
A part of Gale, Cengage Learning

GALE
CENGAGE Learning™

Detroit • New York • San Francisco • New Haven, Conn • Waterville, Maine • London

Christine Nasso, *Publisher*
Elizabeth Des Chenes, *Managing Editor*

© 2011 Greenhaven Press, a part of Gale, Cengage Learning.

Gale and Greenhaven Press are registered trademarks used herein under license.

For more information, contact:
Greenhaven Press
27500 Drake Rd.
Farmington Hills, MI 48331-3535
Or you can visit our Internet site at gale.cengage.com

For product information and technology assistance, contact us at

Gale Customer Support, 1-800-877-4253
For permission to use material from this text or product, submit all requests online at
www.cengage.com/permissions

Further permissions questions can be emailed to permissionrequest@cengage.com

Articles in Greenhaven Press anthologies are often edited for length to meet page requirements. In addition, original titles of these works are changed to clearly present the main thesis and to explicitly indicate the author's opinion. Every effort is made to ensure that Greenhaven Press accurately reflects the original intent of the authors. Every effort has been made to trace the owners of copyrighted material.

Cover Image copyright Dimitri Vervitsiotis/Digital Vision/Dimitri Vervitsiotis.

LIBRARY OF CONGRESS CATALOGING-IN-PUBLICATION DATA

Obesity / Scott Barbour, book editor.
     p. cm. -- (Opposing viewpoints)
   Includes bibliographical references and index.
   ISBN 978-0-7377-4978-6 (hardcover) -- ISBN 978-0-7377-4979-3 (pbk.)
   1. Obesity. I. Barbour, Scott, 1963-
   RA645.O23O22 2010
   616.3'98--dc22
                                                          2010004515

Printed in the United States of America
2 3 4 5 6   15 14 13 12 11

ED087

Contents

Why Consider Opposing Viewpoints?

> "The only way in which a human being can make some approach to knowing the whole of a subject is by hearing what can be said about it by persons of every variety of opinion and studying all modes in which it can be looked at by every character of mind. No wise man ever acquired his wisdom in any mode but this."
>
> *John Stuart Mill*

In our media-intensive culture it is not difficult to find differing opinions. Thousands of newspapers and magazines and dozens of radio and television talk shows resound with differing points of view. The difficulty lies in deciding which opinion to agree with and which "experts" seem the most credible. The more inundated we become with differing opinions and claims, the more essential it is to hone critical reading and thinking skills to evaluate these ideas. Opposing Viewpoints books address this problem directly by presenting stimulating debates that can be used to enhance and teach these skills. The varied opinions contained in each book examine many different aspects of a single issue. While examining these conveniently edited opposing views, readers can develop critical thinking skills such as the ability to compare and contrast authors' credibility, facts, argumentation styles, use of persuasive techniques, and other stylistic tools. In short, the Opposing Viewpoints Series is an ideal way to attain the higher-level thinking and reading skills so essential in a culture of diverse and contradictory opinions.

In addition to providing a tool for critical thinking, Opposing Viewpoints books challenge readers to question their own strongly held opinions and assumptions. Most people form their opinions on the basis of upbringing, peer pressure, and personal, cultural, or professional bias. By reading carefully balanced opposing views, readers must directly confront new ideas as well as the opinions of those with whom they disagree. This is not to simplistically argue that everyone who reads opposing views will—or should—change his or her opinion. Instead, the series enhances readers' understanding of their own views by encouraging confrontation with opposing ideas. Careful examination of others' views can lead to the readers' understanding of the logical inconsistencies in their own opinions, perspective on why they hold an opinion, and the consideration of the possibility that their opinion requires further evaluation.

Evaluating Other Opinions

To ensure that this type of examination occurs, Opposing Viewpoints books present all types of opinions. Prominent spokespeople on different sides of each issue as well as well-known professionals from many disciplines challenge the reader. An additional goal of the series is to provide a forum for other, less known, or even unpopular viewpoints. The opinion of an ordinary person who has had to make the decision to cut off life support from a terminally ill relative, for example, may be just as valuable and provide just as much insight as a medical ethicist's professional opinion. The editors have two additional purposes in including these less known views. One, the editors encourage readers to respect others' opinions—even when not enhanced by professional credibility. It is only by reading or listening to and objectively evaluating others' ideas that one can determine whether they are worthy of consideration. Two, the inclusion of such viewpoints encourages the important critical thinking skill of objectively evaluating an author's credentials and bias. This evaluation will illuminate an author's reasons for taking a particular stance on an issue and will aid in readers' evaluation of the author's ideas.

It is our hope that these books will give readers a deeper understanding of the issues debated and an appreciation of the complexity of even seemingly simple issues when good and honest people disagree. This awareness is particularly important in a democratic society such as ours in which people enter into public debate to determine the common good. Those with whom one disagrees should not be regarded as enemies but rather as people whose views deserve careful examination and may shed light on one's own.

Thomas Jefferson once said that "difference of opinion leads to inquiry, and inquiry to truth." Jefferson, a broadly educated man, argued that "if a nation expects to be ignorant and free . . . it expects what never was and never will be." As individuals and as a nation, it is imperative that we consider the opinions of others and examine them with skill and discernment. The Opposing Viewpoints Series is intended to help readers achieve this goal.

David L. Bender and Bruno Leone,
Founders

Introduction

"The stickiness of the childhood obesity problem begins with a simple truth: most of us just don't think our kids are fat."

—Lori Oliwenstein,
an author who specializes in
science and health topics

Americans are concerned about obesity. In an October 2007 Zogby poll, 46 percent of Americans ranked obesity as the number one health issue facing Americans, placing it in first place above cancer (23 percent) and heart disease (12 percent). Similarly, in an annual survey conducted by the University of Michigan C.S. Mott Children's Hospital, adults ranked obesity the top health risk facing children in both 2008 and 2009. In 2008, 35 percent of adults named obesity as children's foremost risk; in 2009, that number had risen to 42 percent, placing obesity ahead of drug abuse, smoking, and bullying as the primary threat to children's health.

Besides being worried about the problem, Americans support efforts to address obesity. In a 2009 survey conducted by the Trust for America's Health and the Robert Wood Johnson Foundation, 83 percent of respondents found the argument for investing in obesity prevention either "somewhat convincing" or "very convincing." In addition, 87 percent found the argument for responding to childhood obesity "somewhat convincing" or "very convincing."

Despite this high level of awareness and concern, Americans remain obese. The rate of obesity in the United States has more than doubled in the past twenty-five years. According to the Centers for Disease Control and Prevention, 26 percent of Americans over the age of twenty-five are obese—36 percent of blacks, 29 percent of Hispanics, and 24 percent of whites. The nation's children are also too heavy. The rate of obesity is 12 percent among children aged two to five, 17 percent among children six to eleven, and 18 percent among children twelve to nineteen. While childhood obesity rates have leveled off in recent years, they remain more than double what they were twenty years ago.

Thus, awareness of obesity—and even an agreement that action is needed to address it—has not led to significant progress. One reason for this failure is the intractable nature of the problem. Once the human body has gained excess weight, it is extremely difficult to shed the pounds. This difficulty is partly due to human physiology: the body is programmed to retain fat and to quickly regain it once it is lost. In response to this dilemma, an entire weight-loss industry has sprung up offering gyms, diet programs, diet pills, and even surgery to remove extra pounds. Meanwhile, the statistics consistently report high rates of obesity.

In addition to human physiology, the social environment reinforces habits that make weight loss difficult. For example, fast-food restaurants—which offer cheap, high-energy, low-nutrition foods—are ubiquitous in U.S. society and bombard the public with ads promoting their delicious offerings. Moreover, adults are more likely to work in office jobs that require little physical activity, while children and teens are increasingly glued to TVs and video games. This combination of fattening foods and inactivity helps to keep obesity at high levels.

One factor that may help keep childhood obesity rates high is parental misperception. While Americans consider obesity to be a problem in the abstract, several studies have found that parents are often oblivious to overweight conditions and obesity in their children. A 2005 British study surveyed parents of overweight and obese children aged three to five. Only 2 percent of parents of overweight children and 17 percent of parents of obese children described their children as overweight. In another study published in the journal *Obe-*

sity Research (now known as simply *Obesity*), only 11 percent of parents of overweight children perceived their children's weight accurately. Parents of overweight children typically underestimated their children's weights. Yet another study published in 2006 in the journal *Pediatrics* found that only 36 percent of parents of overweight children aged two to seventeen perceived a weight problem in their children. One explanation for this failure to recognize the problem may be that overweight and obesity have become normalized. As Lori Oliwenstein of *Time* magazine puts it, "In a society in which obesity is omnipresent, a slightly hefty child looks pretty normal."[1]

While parents often fail to see obesity in their children, doctors are hesitant to address the issue as well. A study published in the journal *Pediatrics* found that doctors diagnosed obesity in fewer than 1 percent of their patients aged two to eighteen, while the rate of obesity in that age group ranges from 12 percent to 18 percent. Parents may not raise the issue with their doctors because they are unaware of the problem, because they feel responsible for causing it, or because they fear that their children will develop body image problems or eating disorders if they are made aware that they have a weight problem. For their part, doctors may be reluctant to raise the issue out of fear of embarrassing their young patients and shaming their parents. Unfortunately, all this hesitation to discuss the topic means that many children are not getting the help they need to control their weight.

Doctors' reticence and parents' obliviousness are just two factors contributing to the problem of childhood obesity. Other causes may include genetics, a poor diet, a lack of exercise, and the drumbeat of food advertising on television. These and other issues are debated by the authors of the viewpoints in *Opposing Viewpoints: Obesity*, under the rubrics of the following chapters: Is Obesity a Serious Problem? What Causes

1. Lori Oliwenstein, "Weighty Issues," *Time*, June 23, 2008.

Obesity? Who Should Take Responsibility for Obesity? and How Can Obesity Be Reduced? Throughout these chapters, the authors argue the complex interplay of cause and effect that makes obesity such a stubborn public health dilemma.

OPPOSING
VIEWPOINTS®
SERIES

CHAPTER 1

Is Obesity a Serious Problem?

Chapter Preface

The body mass index (BMI) is a system of measurement in which a person's height and weight are entered into a formula in order to arrive at a single numerical value. According to the U.S. National Institutes of Health, a BMI of 19 to 24.9 is normal, 25 to 29.9 is overweight, 30 to 39.9 is obese, and 40 and above is extremely obese. By way of illustration, a person who is 5 foot 7 inches tall and weighs 220 pounds has a BMI of 34.5 and is therefore obese. A person who is 5 foot 7 inches tall and weighs 150 pounds has a BMI of 23.5 and is therefore in the normal range.

Some experts are critical of the BMI, arguing that it is a simplistic tool for measuring obesity and health. They point out that a person's BMI does not necessarily reflect the state of their health. A person with a BMI in the overweight or obese category can be healthier than a person with a BMI in the normal range. In fact, one study conducted by researchers at the U.S. Centers for Disease Control and Prevention found that people with a BMI in the overweight category (25 to 29.9) had a lower risk of premature death than those in the normal range (19 to 24.9). These critics contend that rather than focusing on a person's size, doctors should examine their general health, such as their performance on tests to measure heart health.

Other medical experts concede that the BMI is not perfect, but they insist that it is a good general indicator of health. As stated by Peter Wehrwein, the editor of the *Harvard Health Letter*, "The BMI has been shown to correlate well with the amount of fat tissue we're lugging around." Wehrwein and others insist that this excess fat can cause various medical problems that can limit a person's quality of life and result in premature death. According to the U.S. Department of Health and Human Services, obesity increases a person's risk for type

2 diabetes, coronary heart disease, stroke, certain types of cancer, fatty liver disease, and a variety of other health problems. "And the more excess weight we have, the greater the risk for these diseases—and for an early death," Wehrwein concludes.

The validity of BMI is among the issues debated in the following chapter on the seriousness of the problem of obesity in the United States and around the world.

| "*Overweight and obesity are now dramatically on the rise in low- and middle-income countries.*"

Obesity Is a Serious Problem Worldwide

World Health Organization

The World Health Organization (WHO) is the health authority within the United Nations. It is responsible for providing leadership, overseeing research, and developing policies related to health worldwide. In the following viewpoint, WHO reports that obesity is a growing problem around the world. More than 400 million people are obese, the agency states. The causes of this crisis are an increase in fatty, sugary foods and a decrease in exercise, according to WHO.

As you read, consider the following questions:

1. What are two consequences of overweight and obesity cited by WHO?

2. What is the "double burden" of disease described by the author?

3. What are two actions individuals can take to reduce obesity, as stated by WHO?

"Fact Sheet No. 311: Obesity and Overweight," World Health Organization (WHO), September 2006. Reproduced by permission.

Overweight and obesity are defined as abnormal or excessive fat accumulation that may impair health.

Body mass index (BMI) is a simple index of weight-for-height that is commonly used in classifying overweight and obesity in adult populations and individuals. It is defined as the weight in kilograms divided by the square of the height in meters (kg/m2).

BMI provides the most useful population-level measure of overweight and obesity as it is the same for both sexes and for all ages of adults. However, it should be considered as a rough guide because it may not correspond to the same degree of fatness in different individuals.

The World Health Organization (WHO) defines "overweight" as a BMI equal to or more than 25, and "obesity" as a BMI equal to or more than 30. These cut-off points provide a benchmark for individual assessment, but there is evidence that risk of chronic disease in populations increases progressively from a BMI of 21.

The new WHO Child Growth Standards, launched in April 2006, include BMI charts for infants and young children up to age 5. However, measuring overweight and obesity in children aged 5 to 14 years is challenging because there is not a standard definition of childhood obesity applied worldwide. WHO is currently developing an international growth reference for school-age children and adolescents.

Facts about Overweight and Obesity

WHO's latest projections indicate that globally in 2005:

- approximately 1.6 billion adults (age 15+) were overweight;

- at least 400 million adults were obese.

WHO further projects that by 2015, approximately 2.3 billion adults will be overweight and more than 700 million will be obese.

At least 20 million children under the age of 5 years are overweight globally in 2005.

Once considered a problem only in high-income countries, overweight and obesity are now dramatically on the rise in low- and middle-income countries, particularly in urban settings.

What Causes Obesity and Overweight?

The fundamental cause of obesity and overweight is an energy imbalance between calories consumed on one hand, and calories expended on the other hand. Global increases in overweight and obesity are attributable to a number of factors including:

- a global shift in diet towards increased intake of energy-dense foods that are high in fat and sugars but low in vitamins, minerals and other micronutrients; and

- a trend towards decreased physical activity due to the increasingly sedentary nature of many forms of work, changing modes of transportation, and increasing urbanization.

Serious Health Consequences

Overweight and obesity lead to serious health consequences. Risk increases progressively as BMI increases. Raised body mass index is a major risk factor for chronic diseases such as:

- Cardiovascular disease (mainly heart disease and stroke)—already the world's number one cause of death, killing 17 million people each year.

- Diabetes—which has rapidly become a global epidemic. WHO projects that diabetes deaths will increase by more than 50% worldwide in the next 10 years.

- Musculoskeletal disorders—especially osteoarthritis [inflammation of the joints].

- Some cancers (endometrial [of the lining of the uterus], breast, and colon).

Childhood obesity is associated with a higher chance of premature death and disability in adulthood.

Many low- and middle-income countries are now facing a "double burden" of disease:

- While they continue to deal with the problems of infectious disease and under-nutrition, at the same time they are experiencing a rapid upsurge in chronic disease risk factors such as obesity and overweight, particularly in urban settings.

- It is not uncommon to find under-nutrition and obesity existing side-by-side within the same country, the same community and even within the same household.

- This double burden is caused by inadequate pre-natal, infant and young child nutrition followed by exposure to high-fat, energy-dense, micronutrient-poor foods and lack of physical activity.

Largely Preventable Conditions

Overweight and obesity, as well as their related chronic diseases, are largely preventable.

At the individual level, people can:

- achieve energy balance and a healthy weight;

- limit energy intake from total fats and shift fat consumption away from saturated fats to unsaturated fats;[1]

1. Saturated fats come mostly from animal products and are considered less healthy than unsaturated fats, which come mostly from plant foods.

Obesity in the Developing World

In the past 20 years, the rates of obesity have tripled in developing countries that have been adopting a Western lifestyle involving decreased physical activity and over-consumption of cheap, energy-dense food. Such lifestyle changes are also affecting children in these countries; the prevalence of overweight among them ranges from 10 to 25%, and the prevalence of obesity ranges from 2 to 10%. The Middle East, Pacific Islands, Southeast Asia, and China face the greatest threat.

Parvez Hossain, Bisher Kawar, and Meguid El Nahas,
New England Journal of Medicine, *January 18, 2007.*

- increase consumption of fruit and vegetables, as well as legumes [beans], whole grains and nuts;

- limit the intake of sugars; and

- increase physical activity—at least 30 minutes of regular, moderate-intensity activity on most days. More activity may be required for weight control.

The implementation of these recommendations requires sustained political commitment and the collaboration of many stakeholders, public and private. Governments, international partners, civil society and nongovernmental organizations and the private sector have vital roles to play in shaping healthy environments and making healthier diet options affordable and easily accessible. This is especially important for the most vulnerable in society—the poor and children—who have limited choices about the food they eat and the environments in which they live.

Initiatives by the food industry to reduce the fat, sugar and salt content of processed foods and portion sizes, to increase introduction of innovative, healthy, and nutritious choices, and to review current marketing practices could accelerate health gains worldwide.

WHO's Prevention Strategy

Adopted by the World Health Assembly in 2004, the WHO Global Strategy on Diet, Physical Activity and Health describes the actions needed to support the adoption of healthy diets and regular physical activity. The Strategy calls upon all stakeholders to take action at global, regional and local levels and aims to lead to a significant reduction in the prevalence of chronic diseases and their common risk factors, primarily unhealthy diet and physical inactivity.

WHO's work on diet and physical activity is part of the overall WHO chronic disease prevention and control framework of the Department of Chronic Diseases and Health Promotion. The strategic objectives of the department are to: advocate for health promotion and chronic disease prevention and control; promote health, especially for poor and disadvantaged populations; slow and reverse the adverse trends in the common chronic disease risk factors; and prevent premature deaths and avoidable disability due to major chronic diseases.

This work is complemented by that of the Department of Nutrition for Health and Development. The strategic objectives of the department are to promote healthy diets and improve the nutritional status of the population throughout the life course, particularly among the vulnerable. This is achieved by providing support to countries in developing and implementing national intersectoral Food and Nutrition Policies and Programmes to address the double-burden of nutrition-related ill-health, and to contribute to the achievement of the Millennium Development Goals (MDGs).[2]

2. The Millennium Development Goals are eight goals set by the United Nations in an attempt to reduce poverty, AIDS, and other global problems by 2015.

> "With stultifying regularity the media obediently produce some new scare tactic about the 'health risks of obesity' to maintain the public frenzy over weight and dieting."

The Problem of Obesity Is Exaggerated

Amy Winter

In the following viewpoint, Amy Winter disputes the common claim that obesity is an epidemic. She contents that both the extent and the harms of obesity have been exaggerated. Contrary to the claims of many public health experts and the media, there is no clear explanation for why fat people are fat, and there's no evidence that fat people are unhealthy. Amy Winter is a writer for Off Our Backs, *a news journal by, for, and about women.*

As you read, consider the following questions:

1. According to the author, what is the death rate of surgical procedures for weight loss?

2. Who developed the four principles that have been adopted as the Health At Every Size (HAES) movement, according to Winter?

Amy Winter, "The Biggest Losers & the Lies They Feed Us," *Off Our Backs*, November–December 2004, pp. 17–19. Reproduced by permission.

3. How does the author describe the argument for the "obesity epidemic?"

I have a love-hate relationship with television; as a radical fat feminist, the mainstream values paraded across the screen make steam come out of my ears, but often a state of horrified fascination prevents me from tearing my eyes away. This happened most recently with NBC's "The Biggest Loser," the latest in the series of mainstream mind candy like "Extreme Makeover," "I Want a Famous Face," and "The Swan." Unlike the latter shows, where participants go under the knife, the transformations on "The Biggest Loser"—a show where fat people compete to lose the most weight, while being coached by "celebrity trainers" and tempted by "disallowed" foods—are left to willpower and self-denial.

Misinformation About Weight and Dieting

"The Biggest Loser" is completely dependent on the assumptions and misinformation about weight and dieting that saturate mainstream media, reinforced by the increasing hysteria about the "obesity epidemic." The argument goes something like this: Fat people are fat because they eat too much and lay around all day, and fat is ugly, plus unhealthy! If fat people just worked out and didn't eat so much, they could become thin and beautiful like the rest of us, and all their problems would be solved. A *People Magazine* article speculating on the motivation behind the makeover-show trend states, "As obesity becomes an epidemic and fully two-thirds of all Americans are overweight, authentically slim, good-looking people are becoming rarer and rarer. In other words, we are in the throes of a beauty shortage. And we have applied our typically optimistic, boot-strap attitude to the situation: If we can't grow pretty people, we'll make them. What used to be solely a function of luck can now actually be an accomplishment, something earned through hard work and persistence."

Enter "The Biggest Loser." Despite the supposed ugliness of fat people, the participants on this show seem to have been chosen for their good looks, and their curves in the form-fitting tank tops and shorts they wear throughout the program are very appealing. As I watch the show, I realize how unusual it is to see really fat bodies on television. However, neither participant nor viewer can be allowed to appreciate their appearance as it is. The contestants are filmed deriding themselves and their bodies for being weak, ugly, and unhealthy. As part or the first episode, the two teams are made to compete at pulling cars around a track; a camera inside the car focuses on their t-shirts tightening across their bellies and thighs as they squeeze through the car window to take their required turn at the wheel. Rather than a demonstrating the strength of fat people—able to pull a car!—the contest fosters fat hatred by displaying the bodies this culture disparages in vulnerable, uncomfortable positions.

The two teams are supposedly on "opposing" diet plans the "Eat More Diet" and the "Eat Less Diet." However, reading over the sample menus makes it clear that these diets are hardly different. They are both low-carbohydrate diets, the current fad: they both rely on the same processed "diet" foods like fat-free cold cuts and gelatin packs sweetened with potentially toxic chemical sweeteners. Ultimately, the "Eat More Diet" probably provides only a few hundred calories more per day than the "Eat Less Diet." In short, neither is a program that will teach people how to nourish themselves with real food. One participant is reduced to tears, the diet plan has so confused her about food intake; she believes that eating less than 600 calories a day "can't be enough," but the program has clearly made her doubt herself. Participants berate each other for their food choices and conspire against those who are seen to be eating "too much"; a very thin physical trainer shouts in their faces as they undergo excessive, exhausting, apparently painful workouts. Yet in this environment of intense

No Obesity Catastrophe

Instead of measured debate, what people are hearing is a chorus of obesity alarmism. There's another side to the obesity story. Argued with varying degrees of fervor by epidemiologists, skeptics and sundry others, it points out the arbitrary nature of the body mass index (BMI) classifications, throws doubt on attempts to link high BMI and premature death, asks who stands to gain from the fanning of obesity fears, and questions the value of hounding populations to lose weight. "In general, we just don't know what the long-term consequences of rising obesity are going to be," says [Australian] academic Michael Gard, coauthor with Jan Wright of *The Obesity Epidemic: Science, Morality and Ideology.* "But is it the looming, drop-everything health catastrophe that we're told it is? We say no."

Daniel Williams, Time,
September 11, 2006.

physical activity and limited food intake, a 400-pound man is criticized for eating six pieces of bacon when given the opportunity. Underlying all the interactions between the participants is the assumption that body weight is completely subject to manipulation of food intake and exercise; I want to cry as I experience viscerally the expectation that these fat people can control their own body size. As the show ends, the contestants line up to be weighed; their hope that they will be judged worthy is practically visible as we learn that on this extreme, punishing, self-denying, ultimately unsustainable regimen, some participants have lost over 20 pounds in *one week* all in the quest for "health," of course.

Some Simple Common Sense

But let's apply some simple common sense to the conventional attitude toward weight that "The Biggest Loser" promotes. Given the vast array of weight-loss diets that have made the rounds since the 1950s, you'd think fat would be a thing of the past, wouldn't you? Surprise, surprise—diets don't work. And in a stroke of capitalist genius, the diet industry has not only made billions of dollars selling us products that don't work, they've convinced us that it's *our fault!* If we only had more willpower, we'd be thin—we have no one to blame but ourselves. But just in case we were thinking of resisting wasting money on diets, with stultifying regularity the media obediently produce some new scare tactic about the "health risks of obesity" to maintain the public frenzy over weight and dieting. So, once more, with feeling, a summary of the current state of medical knowledge about fat:

- There's no clear explanation for why fat people are fat. The *New England Journal of Medicine* calls fat people "ordinary people who happen to be heavier than average, probably from some mixture of nature, nurture, and choice."

- There's no known method for fat people to permanently lose weight. The few studies that follow dieters long-term demonstrate failure rates between 85% and 95% for all diets studied; often participants gain back more weight than was lost.

- There's no evidence that fat people are unhealthy. There are no diseases that only fat people get, and there are many diseases that fat people get at lower rates than thin people. Furthermore, people with diabetes, hypertension, and other so-called "obesity-related" diseases often have better blood sugar and blood pressure readings with lifestyle changes that cause little to no weight loss, suggesting that fat itself is not the cause of these problems. In fact, the world's largest study to date found the highest life expectancy in the group of people 60–75 pounds overweight by current U.S. government standards.

- Weight loss itself may have unknown health risks. Since no studies have taken into consideration the fact that most fat people have a life history of dieting, they've failed to control for the possible negative effects of alternating starving and binging, and losing and regaining weight multiple times.

- Weight loss methods such as diet pills and surgery have documented negative side effects and risks, including the risk of death. Surgical procedures for weight loss, such as intestinal bypass (now mostly phased out due to severe complications), gastric bypass and gastroplasty (stomach stapling) can have serious complications, including a death rate of up to 10%; follow-up surgeries are often required to correct hernias or to drain intra-abdominal abscesses. In a recent study, 39% of patients undergoing weight loss surgery were readmitted due to complications from their procedures. After surgery, patients are dependent on protein, vitamin, and mineral supplements for life, and may suffer from diseases like beriberi, which are normally found only in the severely undernourished.

Health at Every Size

This information is not new. Feminists have been critiquing the diet industry, the medical system, and mainstream ideas about body size and weight loss for decades. In an article written in the 1970s, Vivian Mayer exposed the biases and conflicts of interest inherent in research on body size, and suggested the need for a paradigm shift.

Fortunately, some researchers and health practitioners have begun to heed the call. Dietitian Karin Kratina developed four principles that have been adopted as the Health At Every Size (HAES) movement. HAES advocates leaving behind the focus on weight; instead, we're encouraged to abandon attempts at weight loss and accept that healthy bodies come in different sizes. HAES encourages us to eat simple, unprocessed foods as much as we can rather than processed diet foods, to eat when we're hungry and stop when we're full, and to engage in physical movement that we enjoy for its own sake, rather than forcing ourselves into strenuous, regimented workouts with weight loss as a goal. And, unlike diet plans, pills, shakes, and weight loss surgery, these suggestions do not stigmatize or penalize fat people; they constitute a lifestyle that encourages all of us to be as healthy as we can be. The HAES movement has great potential to break the assumed connection between thinness and good health; it's simple, gentle and encourages all people to make healthy food and exercise choices while loving ourselves and our bodies, rather than punishing ourselves with diets and workouts under the mistaken assumption that we can control our body size.

> "Excessive fat ... [traps] the body in a vicious cycle. Even slightly overweight people can be on the path to a disturbed physiology."

Obesity Is Harmful to Human Health

Sarah Baldauf

In the following viewpoint, Sarah Baldauf summarizes the latest research on the effects that excessive fat has on the human body. She explains that far from being a benign substance, fat functions like a gland that secretes hormones that affect many organs in the body. According to Baldauf, too much fat can disrupt the cells' chemical processes and contribute to disorders such as type 2 diabetes, cardiovascular disease, and liver damage. Baldauf is an associate editor for U.S. News & World Report *and writes frequently on health issues.*

As you read, consider the following questions:

1. How does excess fat cause type 2 diabetes, as explained by Baldauf?

Sarah Baldauf, "Too Fat? No More Excuses; Research Is Revealing How Very Damaging Extra Baggage Is," U.S. News & World Report, vol. 144, January 14, 2008, p. 57. Copyright © 2008 U.S. News & World Report, L.P. All rights reserved. Reprinted with permission.

2. What six types of cancer does obesity contribute to, according to the author?

3. Why is deep belly fat especially harmful to the liver, as reported by the author?

You may think your jiggling spare tire is just along for the ride, an inert mass that slows you down and forces a slackened belt. But far from just sitting there quietly, your body fat is talking. And what it's saying—in a constant stream of messages to your brain, liver, muscles, and points in between—amounts to an urgent reason to finally follow through on that New Year's resolution.

Researchers worried about the obesity epidemic are furiously studying body fat in an effort to decode its effect on health. And they have discovered that fat is as active and important an endocrine organ [an organ that produces secretions that are distributed in the body via the bloodstream] as the thyroid or reproductive glands. In healthy amounts, it tightly regulates the amount of energy burned or stored by releasing a cadre of hormones. In excess, the fat cells swell and multiply, and their functioning overwhelms the system: Nasty inflammatory factors spew into the bloodstream, and the delicate balance of hormones becomes skewed, altering the brain's normal response to fat's signals. The result: a much-elevated risk of diabetes, cardiovascular disease, cancer, and liver disease. Plus metabolic changes that make losing weight—and keeping it off—seem impossibly tough.

"People think obesity is two behaviors: gluttony and sloth," says Robert Lustig, director of the Weight Assessment for Teen and Child Health [WATCH] Clinic at the University of California–San Francisco Children's Hospital. "That's not what it is. Obesity is a manifestation of a biochemical problem." Excessive fat strengthens the dysfunction, too, trapping the body in a vicious cycle. Even slightly overweight people can be on the path to a disturbed physiology—no matter that their clothes can still disguise a paunch.

Diabetes

For evidence, look no further than the recent surge in type 2 diabetes, which correlates in near lockstep with Americans' expanding waistlines. As fat stores go up, so does the pancreas's production of insulin, the hormone that helps usher glucose [a type of sugar] out of the bloodstream and into cells where it's used for fuel. So people with too many extra pounds end up with a glut of the stuff, typically leading to "insulin resistance"—and too much glucose in the blood. Meantime, the excess insulin sends energy into the fat cells, causing them to plump up and multiply ad infinitum—and end up in places fat shouldn't be, like muscles, the liver, and deep in the gut, wrapped around vital organs.

Insulin resistance has been Jesse Manek's nemesis. Now 15, Manek was told three years ago that—seriously overweight at 283 pounds and prediabetic—he would very likely have full-blown diabetes or a heart attack by the time he reached his 20s. Manek, who lives in Novato, Calif., sought help from Lustig and the WATCH clinic and has managed to drop more than 75 pounds and bring his body-mass index, a number that relates weight to height, from 41.6 to a closer-to-normal 29.9. His regimen has been ultradisciplined: at least four classes per week at Marin Mixed Martial Arts, weekly sessions of strength training with a personal trainer, and a diet nearly devoid of fructose (found in table sugar and high-fructose corn syrup) and chock-full of fruits, vegetables, and whole grains. Lustig also has treated Manek with metformin, a diabetes drug, to rein in his insulin-gone-haywire. "It really comes down to a mental battle," Manek says of his struggle. "Do you want to be healthy?" He's now safely out of the prediabetic zone.

Besides upsetting the insulin balance, too much fat seems to unleash a flood of molecules called cytokines that trigger systemwide inflammation. "Obesity is a pro-inflammatory state," says Michael Charlton, medical director of liver transplantation at the Mayo Clinic in Rochester, Minn. Normally, inflammation is a healthy immune response, critical to fighting off infection. But chronic inflammation causes widespread tissue damage. The plumper and more abundant a person's fat cells, the greater the number of cytokine-releasing macrophage cells [cells that destroy invaders such as bacteria and viruses] in the fat tissue. "It's these macrophages that are causing a lot of the trouble," says Rudolph Leibel, a Columbia University geneticist and noted obesity researcher. "They make mischief related to how fat you are."

The Cardiovascular System

The cardiovascular system appears to be one victim. Macrophages play an important role in the development of the fatty plaques that lead to atherosclerosis [hardening of the arteries]. And cytokines can make tissues resistant to the effects of insulin and cause inflammation in the blood vessels. Meantime, too much insulin can promote salt retention—and soaring blood pressure. "If I hadn't lost the weight when I did, they say [I'd have had] a heart attack or stroke," says Sheri Fanning, 41, a geriatric care manager and now weight-loss coach in Sparta, Wis., who has heart disease in her family and recently experienced a dangerous blood pressure spike.

Five years ago, Fanning tipped the scale at 192 pounds, and her doctor delivered an ultimatum: Go on hypertension meds for life. Instead, Fanning credits a physician-directed program that offered thrice-weekly weigh-ins, counseling, and a calorie-restricted diet for helping her to get down to a healthy 130 pounds. Taking up marathoning, triathlon, and competitive road biking certainly did its part, too. Though she's been on blood pressure medication since her recent cri-

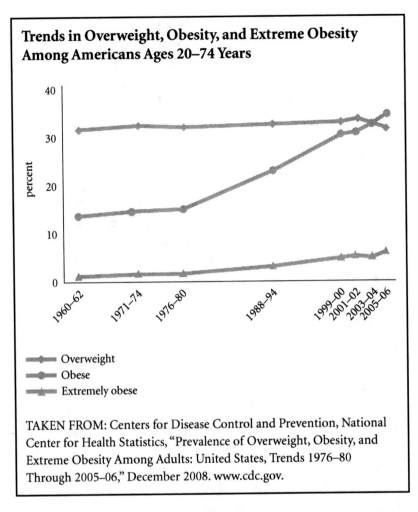

Trends in Overweight, Obesity, and Extreme Obesity Among Americans Ages 20–74 Years

Legend:
- Overweight
- Obese
- Extremely obese

TAKEN FROM: Centers for Disease Control and Prevention, National Center for Health Statistics, "Prevalence of Overweight, Obesity, and Extreme Obesity Among Adults: United States, Trends 1976–80 Through 2005–06," December 2008. www.cdc.gov.

sis, she was able to keep her numbers down for years without drugs; her doctors say that shedding those pounds and keeping them off probably saved her life.

Cancer

Cancer experts, too, now strongly advise burning excess fat. In fact, the top recommendation in the new cancer prevention guidelines issued by the American Institute for Cancer Research and the World Cancer Research Fund puts it this way: "Be as lean as possible within the normal range of body weight." That means keeping your body-mass index between 21 and 23—or, for someone who is 5 foot 4, staying between 122 and 134 pounds. "A BMI of 25 increases the risk of post-menopausal breast cancer more than [a BMI] of 21," says Meir Stampfer, who researches nutrition and epidemiology at the Harvard School of Public Health. Extra fat is strongly believed to raise the risk of six types of cancer—esophageal, pancreatic, colorectal [of the colon and rectum], breast (in postmenopausal women), endometrial [of the mucous membrane lining the uterus], and kidney—and possibly gallbladder cancer, too.

The mechanisms that link obesity and cancer are not known, but the usual suspects—insulin resistance and inflammation—are likely players. Research released at [the December 2007] American Association for Cancer Research conference on cancer prevention found that women with diabetes are 1.5 times more likely to develop colorectal cancer than those who aren't diabetic. "It's possible that fairly high levels of insulin—higher than seen in the prediabetics—are necessary to encourage cancer growth," says Andrew Flood, an epidemiologist at the University of Minnesota. And cytokines released from fat tissue are known to promote tumor growth and cell death.

Damaging the Liver

The workhorse of the body takes a beating, too. For example, when a person carries a surplus of fat, the liver—which is responsible for the breakdown of insulin, sugars, hormones, and lipids [fats]—less effectively produces a protein that helps move fat out. So most chronic overeaters end up with fat stored in this organ. Nonalcoholic fatty liver disease, when severe, results in rampant inflammation and scarring and is projected to be the most common reason for liver transplant by 2020.

"I probably had a week to live," says Bill Mackey, an engineer in Rochester, Minn., who once weighed 350 pounds and got a transplant in 2003 after developing liver failure. Through a yearlong recovery and adjustment to antirejection drugs, Mackey, 60, dropped down to 225 pounds, though he has crept back up to 275 these days. His doctor says this is typical in such patients, as is some reaccumulation of fat in the liver. "That tells you this is not a liver problem," explains Mayo's Charlton. "It's a whole-body problem, an endocrine problem associated with hormones, overnutrition, and some susceptibility factor we're still trying to identify."

Deep belly fat, also known as visceral fat, may especially endanger the liver. "Having fat in that visceral area can potentially increase the flow of fatty acids to the liver and have a next-door-neighbor effect," says Elizabeth Parks, associate professor and expert on liver metabolism at University of Texas Southwestern Medical Center in Dallas. And "maybe the visceral fat is releasing more cytokines [than fat stored elsewhere]." Genes seem to determine—at least in part—where a person stores fat, so lean people aren't necessarily off the hook if they don't exercise or eat a healthful diet.

Hard to Lose

All this new research on the workings of body fat also has revealed why it's so hard to lose weight and keep it off: As you eat more, exercise less, and ratchet upward on the scale, your hormones adjust and fiercely guard the new status quo. For example, the amount of leptin—a hormone secreted by fat that regulates food intake and energy expenditure—circulating in your blood is proportional to the amount of fat you've got stored, says Christopher Newgard, director of the Sarah Stedman Nutrition and Metabolism Center at Duke University. When the hypothalamus [an area of the brain] of a person at a healthy weight sees a higher level of leptin than it expects, it tells the body to ease up on food intake and boost energy burning. Sounds great—perhaps you'd like to sprinkle some on your morning cereal? But researchers tested the supplement idea after leptin was discovered in 1994 and found that chronically high levels seem to desensitize the brain, so that leptin's ability to reduce food intake all but disappears.

Fat cells, moreover, don't seem to go away; while other cells are programmed to die, "you've bought them for life," says Robert Kushner, professor of medicine and obesity-care specialist at Northwestern University Feinberg School of Medicine. Thus, the goal of shedding pounds really is about slimming fat cells down, then keeping them from packing in triglycerides [blood fats] again.

Diet and Exercise

The obvious question: How much work is necessary to succeed at trimming the fat? The American Heart Association and the American College of Sports Medicine issued an updated, joint set of guidelines in August [2007] on physical activity. To "promote and maintain health," 30 minutes of moderate activity five days per week will do the job. But to prevent weight gain or shed pounds, "more is better." In fact, much more is called for: from 60 to 90 minutes of physical activity on most days.

The amount and type of food you take in matter, too, of course—although researchers don't yet understand how (or how well) various diets and interventions work. At Duke, for example, multiple ways of shedding pounds are being studied—from the Atkins Diet to bariatric [gastric bypass] surgery to drug treatments—to clarify what they do to a person biochemically and why certain people have success and others flounder. The one trick that researchers can agree upon so far is both simple and painfully familiar: Eat less and move more.

For Jesse Manek, that meant ditching what he craved most: fast food, ice cream, and sugary foods. In his doctor's mind, the ever present sweetener fructose, which shows up in everything from pasta to sports drinks to soda to breads, is the refined carbohydrate most culpable in the rise of obesity. Its breakdown in the liver, says Lustig, promotes inflammation, hypertension, and insulin resistance. The extra fiber Manek gets by stocking up on fruits, vegetables, and whole grains helps control his insulin levels and makes him feel fuller, longer. Thanks to his vigorous exercise regimen, he says, an irony has unfolded: "I actually eat more now."

| *"The so-called 'overweight' [body mass index] range doesn't . . . correlate with overall increased health risk."*

The Health Harms of Obesity Are Overstated

Paul Campos

In the following viewpoint, Paul Campos argues that the health risks of being overweight have been exaggerated. He focuses on the work of two Harvard researchers, Walter Willett and Meir Stampfer, who Campos says have relied on poor data and have manipulated their results to arrive at skewed conclusions. Rather than causing health harms, Campos states, being at the lower end of the "overweight" range actually decreases a person's risk of death. Campos is a law professor at the University of Colorado in Boulder and the author of The Obesity Myth, *which has also been published as* The Diet Myth.

As you read, consider the following questions:

1. What were the results of Katherine Flegal's research, according to Campos?

Paul Campos, "Thinner: Why Harvard Wants You to Be Unhealthily Thin," *New Republic,* September 10, 2007. Reproduced by permission of *The New Republic.*

2. What percentage of studies have found little or no mortality risk to being overweight, as reported by the author?

3. What is "data dredging" or "data trimming," as defined by Campos?

A big problem with elite institutions is that, for years on end, people in such places can abuse their positions by saying things that aren't true, before anyone whose opinion counts notices.

A particularly clear example of this is provided by the Harvard School of Public Health, which for many years has been pushing a phony claim with great success. The story is simple: That it's well-established scientific fact that being "overweight"—that is, having a body mass index [BMI] figure of between 25 and 30—is, in the words of Harvard professors Walter Willett and Meir Stampfer, "a major contributor to morbidity and mortality." This claim has been put forward over and over again by various members of the School of Public Health's faculty, with little or no qualification. According to this line of argument, there's simply no real scientific dispute about the "fact" that average-height women who weigh between 146 and 174 pounds, and average-height men who weigh between 175 and 209 pounds, are putting their lives and health at risk. Furthermore, according to Willett, such people should try to reduce their weights toward the low end of the government-approved "normal" BMI range of 18.5 to 24.9 (the low end of the range is 108 and 129 pounds for women and men respectively).

Opposite of the Truth

It's difficult to exaggerate the extent to which the actual scientific evidence fails to support any of this. In fact, the current evidence suggests that what the Harvard crew is saying is not merely false, but closer to the precise opposite of the truth.

For the most part, the so-called "overweight" BMI range doesn't even correlate with overall increased health risk. Indeed "overweight," so-called, often correlates with the lowest mortality rates. (This has led to much chin-scratching over the "paradox" of why "overweight" people often have better average life expectancy and overall health than "normal weight" people. The solution suggested by Occam's Razor[1]— that these definitions make no sense—rarely occurs to those who puzzle over this conundrum). Furthermore, it's simply not known if high weight increases overall health risk, or is merely a marker for factors, most notably low socio-economic status, which clearly do cause ill health. As Adam Drewnowski, director of the Center for Public Health Nutrition and a professor of epidemiology and medicine at the University of Washington, told me, "nobody wants to talk about the 'C' word—class. Yet it's clear that social economic gradient is a profound confounding variable in all this, and one that most current studies do not adequately take into account." Moreover, as we shall see, the notion that so-called "overweight" people should try to become very thin, i.e., should try to move into the low end of the "normal" BMI range, is, given the actual epidemiological evidence, nothing less than bizarre.

Overweight People Are Less at Risk

In 2005, the Harvardistas were thrown into a panic when a study by Katherine Flegal and others appeared in the *Journal of the American Medical Association* [*JAMA*]. This study found 86,000 excess deaths per year in the United States among so-called "normal weight" people, when compared to so-called "overweight" persons. In other words, "overweight" people had the lowest mortality risk. The Harvard people quickly organized a press conference at which they denounced the study's results, and claimed its authors had failed to take into account smoking and preexisting disease.

1. Occam's Razor is the principle, stated by fourteenth-century logician William of Occam, that the simplest theory explaining existing data is best.

But that clearly wasn't true. The *JAMA* study's authors explicitly stated that they had done calculations excluding smokers and controlling for preexisting disease, and that employing such exclusions in the published results would not have altered the paper's conclusions. They even published supplementary data on the Centers for Disease Control and Prevention's website showing precisely what their results looked like when they controlled for these factors. None of this has made much difference. Two and a half years later, you can read a story in the September [2007] issue of *Scientific American* in which Stampfer and Willett repeat the claim that the *JAMA* study didn't control for smoking and preexisting disease.

The Medical Consensus

When the baselessness of their criticisms of the *JAMA* paper are brought up, the Harvard people fall back on the claim that this is just one study out of thousands, and that almost all the rest support their claims about the dangers of "overweight." This claim is equally false. Far from being unusual, the *JAMA* paper's results mirror the overall state of the medical literature (as the citations in the paper itself make clear). "Most studies actually have produced results closer to the data of Flegal et al.," says Glenn Gaesser, a University of Virginia professor of kinesiology [the study of human movement]. Gaesser recently undertook a survey of papers published in 2007 that reported data on the relationship between BMI and life expectancy. The vast majority—around 80%—found either no elevated mortality risk associated with "overweight," or the lowest mortality in the "overweight" range.

In particular, it's difficult to find studies in which mortality at the lower end of the "normal" range isn't quite a bit higher than at the low end of the "overweight" range (the absolute low point in the mortality curve tends to be at the border between "normal weight" and "overweight," or in first

Fat and Happy

There is a side to America's weightiness that, while not generally discussed, is worth considering: Moderately overweight people tend to be happier than lighter folks. Indeed, according to data from the University of Michigan and Indiana University's Center on Philanthropy, people in the overweight category in 2001 were 11% less likely than those in the normal range to say they felt inconsolable over the past month. They were also 18% less likely to have felt worthless, or to say that "everything was an effort."

Arthur C. Brooks, Wall Street Journal, *February 17, 2007.*

couple of units of the "overweight" range). Thus Willett's claim that people should strive to be in the lower end of the "normal" range flies directly in the face of the actual data.

Problematic Studies

So what evidence do the Harvard people cite? Not surprisingly, their own studies—most frequently the Nurses Health and Physicians Health studies: long-running observational studies featuring over one hundred thousand participants. But these studies also feature a number of serious problems. For one thing, sometimes they produce the "wrong" results. For example, in 2000 Willett co-authored a paper indicating that younger men with BMIs of 25-27 didn't have elevated mortality risk when compared to "normal weight" younger men, and that, among men older than 65, BMI was unrelated to mortality altogether. How does Willett deal with this inconvenient data? By citing it to support the opposite conclusion, as in this quote from a paper he co-authored earlier this year [2007]:

"During the last two decades, accumulating epidemiological data have strongly suggested that overweight and obesity cause premature death." Willett's own work calls that statement into question.

Often, however, the Harvard people publish papers that, unlike most of the medical literature, find a linear relationship between increasing BMI and increasing mortality risk, once one is above the "underweight" range. The authors get these results by using a very suspicious method: they exclude from their analysis most of the deaths in their participant pool. Indeed, it's not unusual for the Harvard group to exclude as many 85% or 90% of the deaths that occur in their studies. Richard Cooper, Chair of the Department of Preventative Medicine and Epidemiology at Loyola-Chicago Medical School, points out that this looks very much like "data dredging" or "data trimming," i.e., running your data with various extreme exclusionary criteria, until you get the "right" results. Furthermore, "They have no real evidence that excluding all these participants is the right thing to do," he told me. "The Harvard people talk a lot about reverse causality [the idea, for example, that people at the low end of the normal BMI range have relatively high mortality rates because of smoking or sickness], but almost all the studies to date indicate that excluding smokers at the low end of the weight scale makes no difference." Needless to say, such criticisms cast a rather ironic light on the Harvard group's ongoing attacks of the *JAMA* paper's authors for not excluding enough participants from their study.

Relying on Poor Data

In addition, Cooper points out that the *JAMA* authors are using a data set—the National Health and Nutrition Examination Study (NHANES) survey—that almost all epidemiologists consider to be far superior to the Harvard participant pools. (Among other things, the NHANES study is calibrated to reflect the demographic makeup of the U.S. population and the participants' actual heights and weights are measured periodically. By contrast, the Harvard studies are based on questionnaires filled out by doctors and nurses). "The NHANES data are a thousand times more reliable than [the] Nurses Health and Physicians Health [studies]," Cooper told me.

Perhaps in part because of the power the Cambridge cabal wields through peer review, grants, and recommendations, few physicians have openly dissented from its conclusions. Not surprisingly, then, much of the criticism the Harvard crew gets comes from people in other fields: from sociologists, political scientists, senior government researchers, and yes, even a law professor or two. Predictably, this leads people like Willett and Stampfer to complain that their critics "aren't doctors." Leaving aside that some of their critics *are* doctors, it's unclear why the opinion of doctors regarding the interpretation of thousands of epidemiological studies should be valued more than those of social scientists whose professional training involves this sort of meta-statistical analysis.

An Epidemic of Misleading Statements

Of course, one reason the Harvard claims are treated with such respect is that they tell people what they want to hear. Their claims dovetail perfectly with social prejudices that declare one can never be too rich or too thin, and with the widespread desire to believe that sickness and death can be avoided if one follows the rules laid down by the appropriate authority figures. Combine these factors with the social cachet wielded by the Harvard name, a willingness to make brazen assertions that run from serious exaggerations to outright lies, and lazy journalism of the "some say the Earth is flat; others claim it's round; the truth no doubt lies somewhere in the middle" type, of which the *Scientific American* article is only the most recent example, and you have a recipe for an epidemic of wildly misleading statements dressed up in the guise of authoritative scientific discourse.

| *"Obesity is a serious health concern for children and adolescents."*

Obesity in Children Is a Serious Problem

Centers for Disease Control and Prevention

In the following viewpoint, the Centers for Disease Control and Prevention (CDC) argues that obesity among children and adolescents in the United States is a serious problem. While rates of childhood obesity have stabilized in recent years, they remain three times as high as they were in the 1970s. This increase in obesity puts children and teens at risk for various health problems, the CDC concludes. The CDC is an agency of the federal government responsible for developing disease prevention, environmental health, and health promotion strategies for the American public.

As you read, consider the following questions:

1. According to the statistics cited by the CDC, what percentage of those aged 12–19 were obese in 2003–2006?

2. What three possible reasons does the CDC give for the role of sugar-sweetened drinks in contributing to childhood obesity?

Centers for Disease Control and Prevention, "Childhood Overweight and Obesity," August 19, 2009. www.cdc.gov.

3. What factors in communities and neighborhoods contribute to childhood obesity, as argued by the CDC?

Obesity is a serious health concern for children and adolescents. Data from National Health and Nutrition Examination Surveys (NHANES) (1976–1980 and 2003–2006) show that the prevalence of obesity has increased: for children aged 2–5 years, prevalence increased from 5.0% to 12.4%; for those aged 6–11 years, prevalence increased from 6.5% to 17.0%; and for those aged 12–19 years, prevalence increased from 5.0% to 17.6%.

Obese children and adolescents are at risk for health problems during their youth and as adults. For example, during their youth, obese children and adolescents are more likely to have risk factors associated with cardiovascular disease (such as high blood pressure, high cholesterol, and Type 2 diabetes) than are other children and adolescents.

Obese children and adolescents are more likely to become obese as adults. For example, one study found that approximately 80% of children who were overweight at age 10–15 years were obese adults at age 25 years. Another study found that 25% of obese adults were overweight as children. The latter study also found that if overweight begins before 8 years of age, obesity in adulthood is likely to be more severe. . . .

Defining Overweight and Obesity

Body mass index (BMI) is a practical measure used to determine overweight and obesity. BMI is a measure of weight in relation to height that is used to determine weight status. BMI can be calculated using either English or metric units. BMI is the most widely accepted method used to screen for overweight and obesity in children and adolescents because it is relatively easy to obtain the height and weight measurements needed to calculate BMI, measurements are non-invasive and BMI correlates with body fatness. While BMI is an accepted screening tool for the initial assessment of body fatness in children and adolescents, it is not a diagnostic measure because BMI is not a direct measure of body fatness.

For children and adolescents (aged 2–19 years), the BMI value is plotted on the CDC [Centers for Disease Control and Prevention] growth charts to determine the corresponding BMI-for-age percentile.

- Overweight is defined as a BMI at or above the 85th percentile and lower than the 95th percentile.

- Obesity is defined as a BMI at or above the 95th percentile for children of the same age and sex.

These definitions are based on the 2000 CDC Growth Charts for the United States and expert committee. A child's weight status is determined based on an age- and sex-specific percentile for BMI rather than by the BMI categories used for adults. Classifications of overweight and obesity for children and adolescents are age- and sex-specific because children's body composition varies as they age and varies between boys and girls.

Trends in Childhood Obesity

Obesity Prevalence Among Low-Income, Preschool-Aged Children 1998–2008

One of 7 low-income, preschool-aged children is obese, but the obesity epidemic may be stabilizing. The prevalence of obesity in low-income two- to four-year-olds increased from 12.4 percent in 1998 to 14.5 percent in 2003 but rose to only 14.6 percent in 2008.

NHANES Surveys (1976–1980 and 2003–2006)

Obesity is a serious health concern for children and adolescents. Data from NHANES surveys (1976–1980 and 2003–2006) show that the prevalence of obesity has increased: for children aged 2–5 years, prevalence increased from 5.0% to

12.4%; for those aged 6–11 years, prevalence increased from 6.5% to 17.0%; and for those aged 12–19 years, prevalence increased from 5.0% to 17.6%.

Contributing Factors

At the individual level, childhood obesity is the result of an imbalance between the calories a child consumes as food and beverages and the calories a child uses to support normal growth and development, metabolism, and physical activity. In other words, obesity results when a child consumes more calories than the child uses. The imbalance between calories consumed and calories used can result from the influences and interactions of a number of factors, including genetic, behavioral, and environmental factors. It is the interactions among these factors—rather than any single factor—that is thought to cause obesity.

Genetic Factors

Studies indicate that certain genetic characteristics may increase an individual's susceptibility to excess body weight. However, this genetic susceptibility may need to exist in conjunction with contributing environmental and behavioral factors (such as a high-calorie food supply and minimal physical activity) to have a significant effect on weight. Genetic factors alone can play a role in specific cases of obesity. For example, obesity is a clinical feature for rare genetic disorders such as Prader-Willi syndrome.[1] However, the rapid rise in the rates of overweight and obesity in the general population in recent years cannot be attributed solely to genetic factors. The genetic characteristics of the human population have not changed in the last three decades, but the prevalence of obesity has tripled among school-aged children during that time.

1. Symptoms of Prader-Willi syndrome include chronic hunger and a slow metabolism, which can lead to life-threatening obesity.

Behavioral Factors

Because the factors that contribute to childhood obesity interact with each other, it is not possible to specify one behavior as the "cause" of obesity. However, certain behaviors can be identified as potentially contributing to an energy imbalance and, consequently, to obesity.

- *Energy intake*: Evidence is limited on specific foods or dietary patterns that contribute to excessive energy intake in children and teens. However, large portion sizes for food and beverages, eating meals away from home, frequent snacking on energy-dense foods and consuming beverages with added sugar are often hypothesized as contributing to excess energy intake of children and teens. In the area of consuming sugar-sweetened drinks, evidence is growing to suggest an association with weight gain in children and adolescents. Consuming sugar-sweetened drinks may be associated with obesity because these drinks are high in calories. Children may not compensate at meals for the calories they have consumed in sugar-sweetened drinks, although this may vary by age. Also, liquid forms of energy may be less satiating than solid forms and lead to higher caloric intake.

- *Physical activity*: Participating in physical activity is important for children and teens as it may have beneficial effects not only on body weight, but also on blood pressure and bone strength. Physically active children are also more likely to remain physically active throughout adolescence and possibly into adulthood.

- Children may be spending less time engaged in physical activity during school. Daily participation in school physical education among adolescents dropped 14 percentage points over the last 13 years—from 42% in

1991 to 28% in 2003. In addition, less than one-third (28%) of high school students meet currently recommended levels of physical activity.

- *Sedentary behavior:* Children spend a considerable amount of time with media. One study found that time spent watching TV, videos, DVDs, and movies averaged slightly over 3 hours per day among children aged 8–18 years. Several studies have found a positive association between the time spent viewing television and increased prevalence of obesity in children. Media use, and specifically television viewing, may

- displace time children spend in physical activities,

- contribute to increased energy consumption through excessive snacking and eating meals in front of the TV,

- influence children to make unhealthy food choices through exposure to food advertisements, and

- lower children's metabolic rate.

Environmental Factors

Home, child care, school, and community environments can influence children's behaviors related to food intake and physical activity.

- *Within the home:* Parent-child interactions and the home environment can affect the behaviors of children and youth related to calorie intake and physical activity. Parents are role models for their children who are likely to develop habits similar to their parents.

- *Within child care:* Almost 80% of children aged 5 years and younger with working mothers are in child care for 40 hours a week on average. Child care providers are sharing responsibility with parents for children during important developmental years. Child care can be a setting in which healthy eating and physical activity habits are developed.

- *Within schools*: Because the majority of young people aged 5–17 years are enrolled in schools and because of the amount of time that children spend at school each day, schools provide an ideal setting for teaching children and teens to adopt healthy eating and physical activity behaviors. According to the Institute of Medicine (IOM), schools and school districts are, increasingly, implementing innovative programs that focus on improving the nutrition and increasing physical activity of students.

- *Within the community*: The built environment within communities influences access to physical activity opportunities and access to affordable and healthy foods. For example, a lack of sidewalks, safe bike paths, and parks in neighborhoods can discourage children from walking or biking to school as well as from participating in physical activity. Additionally, lack of access to affordable, healthy food choices in neighborhood food markets can be a barrier to purchasing healthy foods.

Consequences of Obesity for Children

Childhood obesity is associated with various health-related consequences. Obese children and adolescents may experience immediate health consequences and may be at risk for weight-related health problems in adulthood.

Psychosocial Risks: Some consequences of childhood and adolescent obesity are psychosocial. Obese children and adolescents are targets of early and systematic social discrimination. The psychological stress of social stigmatization can cause low self-esteem which, in turn, can hinder academic and social functioning, and persist into adulthood.

Cardiovascular Disease Risks: Obese children and teens have been found to have risk factors for cardiovascular disease (CVD), including high cholesterol levels, high blood pressure, and abnormal glucose [blood sugar] tolerance. In a population-based sample of 5- to 17-year-olds, 70% of obese children had at least one CVD risk factor while 39% of obese children had two or more CVD risk factors.

Additional Health Risks: Less common health conditions associated with increased weight include asthma, hepatic steatosis, sleep apnea and Type 2 diabetes.

- Asthma is a disease of the lungs in which the airways become blocked or narrowed causing breathing difficulty. Studies have identified an association between childhood obesity and asthma.

- Hepatic steatosis is the fatty degeneration of the liver caused by a high concentration of liver enzymes. Weight reduction causes liver enzymes to normalize.

- Sleep apnea is a less common complication of obesity for children and adolescents. Sleep apnea is a sleep-associated breathing disorder defined as the cessation of breathing during sleep that lasts for at least 10 seconds. Sleep apnea is characterized by loud snoring and labored breathing. During sleep apnea, oxygen levels in the blood can fall dramatically. One study estimated that sleep apnea occurs in about 7% of obese children.

- Type 2 diabetes is increasingly being reported among children and adolescents who are obese. While diabetes and glucose intolerance, a precursor of diabetes, are common health effects of adult obesity, only in recent years has Type 2 diabetes begun to emerge as a health-related problem among children and adolescents. Onset of diabetes in children and adolescents can result in advanced complications such as CVD and kidney failure.

| "Blacks and Hispanics are in worse shape than whites—who, of course, are firmly in the grip of the obesity epidemic themselves."

Obesity Among Minorities Is a Serious Problem

Lenny Bernstein

In the following viewpoint, Lenny Bernstein points out the contrast between the athletic supremacy of some minority athletes and the obesity of many ordinary minorities. He cites statistics showing that the rate of obesity is higher among African Americans and Hispanics and offers some potential causes for this disparity. African Americans have traditionally eaten foods that are high in salt and fat, he maintains. Moreover, minorities are more likely to be poor and therefore have less time and fewer options for exercise. Bernstein writes a column on fitness for the Washington Post.

As you read, consider the following questions:

1. What are the rates of obesity among blacks and Hispanics, according to the Centers for Disease Control and Prevention statistics cited by the author?

2. Why are people less likely to exercise in poor neighborhoods, according to Bernstein?

3. What were the results of NiCole Keith's study on the rates of exercise among poor and moderate-income blacks, as reported by the author?

For a sports fan, this September [2009] is a bit like Christmas. The National Football League (NFL) season is starting, and the speed, power and grace of Minnesota Vikings running back Adrian Peterson is on display. At the U.S. Open, [tennis star] Serena Williams tore through the field as usual, before self-destructing. Baseball is heading toward the playoffs; the superhuman Albert Pujols has a shot at the Triple Crown.[1] The majestic Michael Jordan was inducted into the National Basketball Association (NBA) Hall of Fame, and it won't be long before [basketball stars] Kobe [Bryant] and LeBron [James] are back on the floor.

An Inescapable Irony

Yet here is the irony I couldn't escape as I sat in front of my television last week, taking it all in: The overall fitness level of the minority groups those superstars represent is appalling. By any measure that matters, blacks and Hispanics are in worse shape than whites—who, of course, are firmly in the grip of the obesity epidemic themselves.

According to the Centers for Disease Control and Prevention [CDC], 38.2 percent of whites over the age of 18 did no

1. In baseball, a batter achieves the Triple Crown when at season's end he leads the league in home runs, runs batted in, and batting average. Pujols did not win it in 2009, although he did lead the league in home runs, hitting forty-seven.

physical exercise (outside of work) in 2006. For blacks, the figure was 48.9 percent and for Hispanics it was an astonishing 53.4 percent.

The result of these disparities is sadly easy to predict. Fully 54 percent of African American women older than 20 are obese—not overweight, obese—by CDC standards. For Hispanics, the proportion is 42 percent, and for whites it is 32 percent. In combination with generally poorer diets and less access to medical care, that level of physical inactivity helps explain why minorities suffer proportionately more hypertension, Type 2 diabetes and heart disease. Their life expectancies also are shorter.

A larger percentage of African American and Hispanic children ages 6 to 19 are overweight than their white counterparts.

The reasons for this state of affairs are controversial and—as with all matters of race, income and personal motivation—a difficult subject. We'll get to them in a moment. But I bring this up now for a number of reasons.

Confronting the Crisis

On Wednesday night [September 9, 2009], President [Barack] Obama, a fitness freak, delivered his long-awaited address on overhauling the U.S. health-care system, an effort that all sides agree must place greater emphasis on preventive measures such as improved diet and more exercise. And with summer ending, we'll all soon be spending a lot more time indoors. If you're like me, you'll be packing on the winter pounds.

Yet the approach of autumn also brings us the first annual (and possibly the first-ever) "walk-off" against obesity. On Saturday [September 12, 2009], thousands of people in more than 50 cities assembled against this killer.

The event was organized by Ian Smith, who launched the "50 Million Pound Challenge" in 2007. If you don't watch VH1's "Celebrity Fit Club" or read diet books, you may not

Black Youths: The New Face of Type 2 Diabetes

The increasing rate of type 2 diabetes among children is believed to be a result of the dramatic rise in adolescent obesity, particularly central obesity or belly fat, which has been found to trigger the body to resist insulin.

And nowhere can that weight gain be seen more than in African-American youths. Today, close to 24 percent of African-American children are obese (a 10-year-old child, for example, who is 4-foot-6 is considered to be overweight if he or she weighs more than 97 pounds, according to the Body Mass Index). In fact, the rate of obesity for Blacks is double what it was just two decades ago and twice the rate of White adolescents.

Excessive weight gain coupled with a genetic predisposition for diabetes among African-Americans has made Black youths (ages 10 to 19) the new face of type 2 diabetes.

Kevin Chappel, Ebony, *March 2008.*

recognize "Dr. Ian," as his fans know him. (I'd never heard of him until a colleague mentioned his name.) But among African Americans, the slim, Dartmouth-educated physician is well-known for creating a national organization that has confronted their health problems and enlisted tens of thousands in a bid to lose weight. The group has since branched out and is trying to appeal to all races.

"Listen, the swine flu isn't going to kill a tenth of the people that obesity kills on an annual basis," Smith said in an interview. "This is one of the biggest health concerns for America, and we can't get people to talk about it. . . . The sense of urgency isn't there."

One of the walk sites was in Alexandria, [Virginia,] where Mayor William D. Euille led a team of about 40 people for a 1.5-mile walk. Over the past four years, Euille, an African American, has lost 60 pounds from his 5-foot-9 frame and kept it off.

"I got tired of hearing and reading and seeing obese kids and watching primarily African Americans suffer diabetes and high blood pressure," he said. "My role, being African American, and being leader of this city, [is that] I'm the best person to deliver that message.

"No more excuses," Euille said. "It is as simple as just walking."

Or is it? Here is where experts disagree, and close examination of cultural and environmental factors makes solutions more elusive than they first appear.

Cultural Factors

Yes, obesity is a problem for all races and ethnic groups in this country and, generally speaking, affects people of all income levels. But higher proportions of the poor, minorities and the less educated tend to be obese, research shows.

Start with the traditional African American diet, Smith said, one rich in salty, fried food, a menu that has been handed down over generations. Add a greater acceptance of plus-size bodies by both African American men and women, along with some women's disdain for exercise, and the cultural factors are stacked against blacks, he said.

Poverty and Environment

If you're poor, you may be sacrificing leisure time and exercise to make ends meet. Your grocery store may be stocked with cheaper, less healthful food. You probably have less access to fitness facilities, your neighborhood may not have sidewalks, and the local park may be the place where gangs hang out or drugs are sold, rather than a safe haven for an evening jog.

If you think this is a bunch of liberal excuses, you should know that it is supported by research. David Marquez, an assistant professor in the Department of Kinesiology and Nutrition at the University of Illinois at Chicago, who studies the physical activity levels of Hispanics, cited research showing that many Hispanic women feel that working, caring for their families and running their homes leaves them no leisure time at all.

Older Latinas also suggest that the only appropriate exercise for women is walking or dancing, Marquez said. Which is why he is trying to launch programs that center on dance as the primary form of physical activity.

NiCole Keith, an associate professor of exercise physiology at Indiana University–Purdue University Indianapolis was a researcher on one of the few studies of exercise that controlled for income. Researchers gave poor and moderate-income blacks equal access to fitness resources and—surprise!—they exercised at the same rates. Keith says poverty and environmental factors are unquestionably part of the equation.

"If you live in a dangerous area, you cannot get out and walk and run," she said. "If you say, 'You can walk on your lunch hour,' you're making the assumption that you have a job with a lunch hour. And you're assuming everybody can walk when many morbidly obese individuals simply cannot."

In recent years, Keith has had some success persuading Indianapolis principals to open school facilities after hours in inner-city neighborhoods so that adults and kids can exercise. She and colleagues have led videoconference exercise routines for people too infirm or too large to get outside for a walk. They also have tried adding exercise rooms to public housing projects. Urban planners are being educated on the importance of sidewalks. And the American College of Sports Medicine's Exercise Medicine Campaign calls on policymakers to require doctors to counsel patients on physical activity during primary care visits. "If facilities are available and afford-able or free, people will go," Keith said.

Periodical Bibliography

The following articles have been selected to supplement the diverse views presented in this chapter.

Sarah Baldauf   "The Huge Health Toll Obesity Takes on Kids," *U.S. News & World Report*, July 28, 2009.

Alex Beam   "Who Are You Calling Fat?" *Boston Globe*, September 17, 2009.

Paul Campos   "Don't Feed the Humans," *New Republic*, November 27, 2007.

Kevin Chappel   "Black Youths: The New Face of Diabetes," *Ebony*, March 2008.

R.W. Jeffrey   "Is the Obesity Epidemic Exaggerated? No,"
and N.E. Sherwood   *British Medical Journal*, February 2, 2008.

Jeffrey Kluger   "How America's Children Packed on the Pounds," *Time*, June 23, 2008.

Susan Levine   "Obesity Threatens a Generation," *Washington*
and Rob Stein   *Post*, May 17, 2008.

Kate Lunau   "Size Isn't Everything: New Research Suggests Even Those Who Appear 'Thin on the Outside' Can Be 'Fat on the Inside,'" *Maclean's*, May 18, 2009.

Tare Parker-Pope   "Better to Be Fat and Fit than Skinny and Unfit," *New York Times*, August 19, 2008.

Jacob Sullum   "Fat Chances: Is Overweight the New Healthy?" *Reason*, November 14, 2007.

OPPOSING
VIEWPOINTS®
SERIES

CHAPTER 2

I What Causes Obesity?

Chapter Preface

Most health experts agree that there is no single cause of obesity. Rather, a combination of factors is to blame for the problem. Some people likely carry a genetic predisposition for obesity—that is, due to their genetic makeup, they are more likely than others to become obese. Other factors include an increasingly sedentary lifestyle; people today are more likely to spend their workday sitting at a desk than plowing a field. In addition, people have less time for preparing healthy meals and may lack the money for the ingredients for those meals; therefore, they increasingly rely on cheap foods—such as fast-food restaurant meals—that are high in calories but low in nutrition. All of these causes and others likely contribute to the problem of obesity.

Underlying the various causes of obesity may be one biological imperative: evolution may have conditioned the human body to become obese. In prehistoric times, food was scarce. Those whose bodies were able to conserve energy were more likely to survive and pass this trait on. Therefore, the human body was ingrained with the ability to store energy reserves in the form of fat, thus enabling it to survive times of scarcity between hunts. As explained by Elizabeth Kolbert, a staff writer for the *New Yorker* magazine, "Early humans lived . . . hand to mouth. In good times, they needed to stockpile food for use in hard times, but the only place they had to store it was on themselves. . . . As a consequence, a person with a genetic knack for storing fat would have had a competitive advantage."

However, what was a competitive advantage during prehistoric times may be a liability in modern society. The human body retains the ability to store energy, but for most people this trait is no longer needed; food is cheap, plentiful, and energy-rich, and it is easily obtained with little energy. As stated by pediatrician Jimmy Unger, "Our 'hunt' consists of getting into our car and buying a tasty two-dollar, 2,000-calorie meal from a drive-through window. Now that we no longer depend on an occasional bison kill or a successful harvest of roots and berries, the very same traits that once guaranteed our survival now hurt us."

Evolution cannot fully explain the increase in obesity in recent years. Most likely it is just one piece of the puzzle, along with other factors such as exercise, nutrition, and advertising. These and other issues are debated in the following chapter on the causes of obesity.

| "While a confluence of factors contribute to childhood obesity, advertising and marketing clearly are very significant ones."

Food Advertising Contributes to Obesity

Patti Miller

In the following viewpoint, Patti Miller argues that advertising by fast-food and junk-food companies contributes to the problem of childhood obesity in the United States. According to Miller, children view tens of thousands of TV ads promoting unhealthy food and drink products each year. Because the food and beverage industry has failed to adequately regulate itself, Miller contends, the government should require the media to provide equal time to the promotion of healthy foods. Miller is vice president of the Children and the Media Program at Children Now, a nonprofit organization that promotes public policies that benefit children.

As you read, consider the following questions:

1. What did the 2005 Institute of Medicine report on food advertising recommend, according to the author?

Patti Miller, statement before the Subcommittee on Labor, Health and Human Services, Education, and Related Agencies, United States Senate, from *Watch What You Eat: Food Marketing to Kids*, September 23, 2008. Reproduced by permission.

2. In Miller's view, what loophole allows the food and beverage industry to promote unhealthy food as "better for you"?

3. What loophole is created by the media's failure to take responsibility for the advertising of unhealthy foods, in the author's opinion?

Our nation's children are facing an unprecedented public health crisis. For the first time in modern history, we have a generation of children whose life expectancy may be lower than that of their parents. The U.S. Surgeon General has identified overweight and obesity as "the fastest growing cause of disease and death in America."

While a confluence of factors contribute to childhood obesity, advertising and marketing clearly are very significant ones. Children are exposed to tens of thousands of ads each year on television alone, the majority of which are for fast food, junk food and sugared cereals.

In 2005, the Institute of Medicine [IOM] released a report which found compelling evidence that television advertising influences the food and beverage preferences, purchase requests and consumption habits of children. The IOM recommended that the food industry voluntarily shift advertising and marketing targeted to kids to products and beverages that are lower in calories, fat, salt and added sugars and higher in nutrient content. If the industry was not able to achieve significant reform, the IOM recommended that Congress intervene.

Children Now was hopeful that the industry—both the food/beverage companies and the media companies—would respond to the IOM's call to action. Yet more than two years have already passed and unfortunately, voluntary industry action has fallen considerably short of the goal.

Advertising Promotes Unhealthy Eating

The committee's review indicates that, among many factors, food and beverage marketing influences the preferences and purchase requests of children, influences consumption at least in the short term, is a likely contributor to less healthful diets, and may contribute to negative diet-related health outcomes and risks among children and youth. The literature indicates relationships among marketing, dietary precursors, diets, diet-related health, and, in particular, adiposity (body fatness). . . .

Given the findings from the systematic evidence review of the influence of marketing on the precursors of diet, and given the evidence from content analyses that the preponderance of television food and beverage advertising relevant to children and youth promotes high-calorie and low-nutrient products, it can be concluded that television advertising influences children to prefer and request high-calorie and low-nutrient foods and beverages.

Institute of Medicine,
Food Marketing to Children and Youth:
Threat or Opportunity? *2006.*

An Insufficient Initiative

Industry leaders assert that the Children's Food and Beverage Advertising Initiative, a voluntary self-regulatory program that includes 14 food and beverage companies, has sufficiently addressed the concerns about unhealthy food advertising to children. They tell advocates to give the Initiative a chance to work. Yet the Initiative is insufficient for three main reasons:

- The food/beverage companies participating in the Initiative say they will advertise "healthier products" to children—but the companies lack a uniform nutrition standard for defining healthy foods. This poses numerous problems. It will be confusing to parents. It creates situations where similar food products will be classified as "healthy" for kids by one company but will be considered "unhealthy" for kids by another company's standards. This absence of a level playing field allows companies to maneuver both their product portfolios and their definitions of "better for you" food to best serve their own economic interests. For the industry initiative to effectively address the concerns about childhood obesity, there must be a uniform nutrition standard for defining healthy foods that food/beverage companies adopt.

- Food/beverage companies have created a huge loophole that allows non-nutritious foods to be categorized as "better for you" for children. They take products loaded with added sugar and fat, and then label the item as "better for you" because it has a modest proportion of the unhealthy ingredients removed. It's true that it is "better for you" to eat Fruit Loops or Cocoa Puffs with less sugar than the original formula with all of the added sugar. But it's also true that these types of products remain non-nutritious and that regular consumption poses a risk of obesity. "Better for you" foods are not the same as "healthy" foods. We must close the "better for you" food loophole and focus on the goal of shifting food and beverage advertising to children to actual healthy products.

- Media companies that deliver children's programming are absent from any attempt to solve this problem. They refuse to take the necessary steps to reduce unhealthy food advertising to children. They simply point toward the food and beverage companies, hoping they will fix it. Yet without the participation of media companies, another loophole is created. Food/beverage companies that do not participate in the industry initiative will be allowed to continue to advertise junk food to children. That's hardly a solution to the problem. Media companies must play a critical gatekeeper role by monitoring their advertising environments to ensure that unhealthy food advertising is significantly reduced, while advertising for healthy food products is enhanced.

Because there is no uniform nutrition standard; because unhealthy products creatively labeled as "better for you" are being passed off as healthy food for children; and because the media companies refuse to play a role in protecting children from the advertising of unhealthy food products, all of the public health and child advocacy groups involved with the Joint Senate/Federal Communications Commission (FCC) Task Force [on Media and Childhood Obesity] have refused to accept the industry initiative as a viable solution to the problem we face here.

Equal Time for Healthy Food

Children Now believes that media companies (both broadcast and cable) should be required to devote either equivalent time or a majority of their total advertising time for the promotion of healthy and nutritious food products, as judged by basic scientific standards. To accomplish this, Congress should:

- Adopt legislation mandating that at least 50% of all food advertising to children on broadcast and cable television programming be devoted to healthy food products;

- Delegate to an appropriate agency or agencies the task of devising criteria for a uniform nutrition standard that would identify healthy, nutritious foods.

It is essential that we intervene on behalf of the nation's children. Industry is privileging their profits over the health and nutrition concerns of the nation's children. The stakes are too high to sell children's needs short.

| "Advertising has not caused the obesity
epidemic in America."

Food Advertising Does Not Cause Obesity

Paul Kurnit

In the following viewpoint, Paul Kurnit contends that the food and beverage industry should not be blamed for causing obesity. He argues that while obesity rates have risen in recent decades, spending on food and beverage advertising has actually gone down. In addition, Kurnit states, food companies have taken many steps to make their products healthier and to educate the public about the importance of healthy food choices. Kurnit is a professor of marketing at Pace University's Lubin School of Business.

As you read, consider the following questions:

1. What are two of the many causes of obesity other than advertising cited by the author?

2. What did the 2006 Institute of Medicine report conclude about the link between advertising and obesity, according to Kurnit?

Paul Kurnit, "Art & Commerce: The Advertising Diet," *Adweek*, December 3, 2007. Reproduced by permission.

3. In the author's opinion, what constituencies need to work together to solve the obesity problem?

The obesity epidemic in America started five years ago. The ever-widening problem had been building for some time before that, but in 2003, advocacy groups and politicians sounded the alarm that America was fat and getting fatter. Childhood obesity carries with it staggering risks of disease and huge additional costs for medical care.

The obesity outcry of a few years ago was squarely pointed at the food and advertising industries. The simple and pervasive problem, it was claimed, was that food companies were making bad-for-us foods and advertising was causing obesity. If only the problem was that simple, there could likely be a simple solution. But, alas, it just wasn't, it just isn't, the case. In fact, more than 80 percent of parents believe that if their kids are overweight, they are to blame.

Caught Off Guard

The major food companies, at first, were caught completely off guard by the criticism. Their initial response was "what did we do wrong?" The foods and related advertising promoting them have been part of the American diet for well over 50 years. Baby boomers grew up with presweetened cereal and fast food. Product development and advertising practice have essentially gone unchanged. There are more products and choices, to be sure. The media marketplace has also changed dramatically. But, food and beverage advertising dollars targeting children are down, not up.

The obesity problem is certainly real, though. It is a complex multi-dimensional issue. The commitment to and budgets for physical education in schools are way down. After-school sports programs have been cut. No one knows what a portion size should be. The food pyramid went from outdated to an update that is so confusing we don't know what an appropriate eating regimen is. Today's parents are afraid to send their kids outside after school to run around. Many moms are so busy they don't have or make the time to cook complete, well-balanced meals for dinner. Everybody's running to the next activity, but too few of us are running for health and wellness. The solution is energy balance: Burn the calories we consume. We are surely out of balance, but food and beverage advertising has nothing to do with that.

The Institute of Medicine 2006 report "Food Marketing to Children and Youth: Threat or Opportunity?" examined every food study conducted in America and found no linkage between advertising and obesity. Advertising informs children about food and beverage brand options, but it does not proscribe quantity or calorie content kids consume.

Industry Efforts

That notwithstanding, the food companies and advertising agencies got the wake-up call. Frito-Lay removed trans fats from all of its snack products long before New York Mayor Mike Bloomberg even considered the issue. Parent company PepsiCo created a Smart Spot program and issued a corporate edict that a minimum of 50 percent of the company's new products had to fulfill better-for-you food criteria. General Mills reformulated its cereals to use whole grains and altered advertising guidelines to depict its foods in complete and appropriate meal or snacking contexts. Kraft introduced 100-calorie packs, a new line of South Beach Diet products, stated it would no longer advertise its high-fat or sugar products to children and created a new Sensible Solutions program. McDonald's extended a line of salads and revised its Happy Meals to include a choice of skim milk or Apple Dippers in place of soft drinks and fries. Virtually overnight, McDonald's became the largest purchaser of apples in the United States. Other proactive company initiatives in food and advertising practice are being implemented at a dizzying pace.

The corporate actions by the food companies have been dramatic in their range, scope and speed. In a business where new product introductions and corporate policy can take years to implement, market change and impact have moved at light speed. And still the major food companies are under siege. There is a fundamental distrust that they are committed to doing well by doing good. They are. It's a new age. Self-regulation and a new Children's Food and Beverage Advertising Initiative launched by the Council of Better Business Bureaus are working actively and effectively to encourage and realize new marketing practices in health and wellness.

Concerted Action Is Needed

The solution to the obesity crisis is not simple. It will require a wide range of constituencies to pull together to inspire social change—parents, teachers, government, industry and kids themselves. Industry is doing its part. It can and will do more. But, saber-rattling lawsuits and threatened regulation are not the solution. They polarize parties who need to work together to achieve concerted joint action for positive change.

To be sure, advertising is a powerful communications form. And youth are powerful ambassadors for social movements. The pervasive adoption of seat-belt usage in this country happened not because of laws, but because kids urged parents to buckle up. The designated driver is a teen initiative that has tremendously reduced drunken driving among youth. Both were promoted through Advertising Council efforts, but both were adopted and evangelized by youth. Word of mouth, the kid buzz network, is the most powerful form of advertising today.

So it can be, should be and will be for health and wellness. Advertising has not caused the obesity epidemic in America, but it can be a major part of the solution to the problem. We need more, not less advertising messaging to kids about good foods, healthy diet, exercise and energy balance. New proactive

Food Industry Committed to Change

In November 2006, the Better Business Bureau (BBB) launched the new children's food and beverage advertising self-regulation program with 10 leading food and beverage companies that had joined with the BBB to establish the Children's Food and Beverage Advertising Initiative (CFBAI). The goal of the CFBAI is to shift the mix of advertising messaging directed to children under 12 to encourage healthier dietary choices and healthy lifestyles. Accordingly, this program uniquely focuses on the nutritional profile of the food and beverage products featured in advertising primarily directed to children under 12.

On July 18, 2007, the BBB announced the commitments or "pledges" of the then 11 participants at a joint Federal Trade Commission (FTC)/Health and Human Services (HHS) Forum, "Weighing In: A Check-Up on Marketing, Self-Regulation, and Childhood Obesity." Since then two additional leading companies have joined the program and the BBB has approved and announced their pledges. Collectively, at the time the program began the participants represented a substantial portion of child-directed food and beverage advertising. Specifically, they represented at least two-thirds of the television advertising expenditures for food and beverage advertising to children in 2004.

Council of Better Business Bureaus,
"The Children's Food & Beverage Advertising
Initiative in Action," July 2008.

advertising to engage and inform our youth about the dynamics of wellness can empower kids to drive a new social movement as the ambassadors for a healthier America.

| "Farm subsidies create real problems for the average American eater."

American Farm Subsidies Contribute to Obesity

Julie Gunlock

In the following viewpoint, Julie Gunlock argues that American farm subsidies contribute to the problem of obesity in America. These policies give farmers a financial incentive to grow massive quantities of corn, she explains, and much of this corn is used to produce the sweetener high-fructose corn syrup (HFCS). Because HFCS is cheaper than other types of sugar, food companies use it routinely in many of their products, leading to higher rates of obesity and other health problems, Gunlock maintains. Gunlock is a senior fellow at the Independent Women's Forum, a conservative public policy research organization.

As you read, consider the following questions:

1. What proportion of products in the grocery store contains corn derivatives, according to Gunlock?

2. How much more expensive are cane and beet sugar in the United States than in other nations, as reported by the author?

Julie Gunlock, "Eating Is No Fun Anymore," *National Review Online*, August 7, 2009. Reproduced by permission.

3. Why do families choose to consume HFCS-laden foods and sodas, in Gunlock's opinion?

It's depressing when formerly pleasurable pursuits become hot-button political topics: Suddenly your normal trip for a burger and fries becomes a question of morality, life, and death. Are those French fries prepared in heart-healthy olive or canola oil? Is that beef humanely raised and slaughtered, and should I even eat beef when there's a super-delicious veggie burger on the menu? Are the onion, lettuce, and tomato toppings locally sourced and certified organic? Are the pickles made "in house," the mustard by grinding mustard seeds with a mortar and pestle?

It is all so exhausting. It makes me just want to stop eating altogether.

It was with this attitude that I went to an afternoon showing of *Food Inc.* I was fully prepared to hate it, expecting another lecture from the food police, another horror story about fast food. I even entered the theater empty-handed—no popcorn or candy. I was ready to be grossed out.

To my surprise, I actually liked most of it. It had melodramatic moments, and the predictable "big business is bad" message became rather tiresome a half-hour into the movie, but there were—to use a popular Obamaism [a phrase used by President Barack Obama]—some teachable moments in the movie and even a compelling political message too few have heard before: Farm subsidies create real problems for the average American eater.

Corn Is Everywhere

Farm subsidies have been around for so long that only octogenarians have lived in a food subsidy–free America. The first subsidies—introduced by Pres. Franklin D. Roosevelt in the 1930s—were marketed to the American public as a "temporary solution" to help the collapsing farm industry. Some 70 years later, it appears the United States is still in the recovery phase.

Food Inc. boils the subsidy issue down to the basics: Farm subsidies artificially reduce the cost of some food—mainly manufactured and unhealthy snack foods—and create incentives for farmers to produce massive amounts of some commodities no single nation can possibly absorb.

So, what happens? Well, as *Food Inc.* demonstrates with the help of an upbeat soundtrack and colorful pop-up images of ketchup bottles and batteries, people start getting pretty creative with how to put those commodities to use. Enter corn—lots of corn.

U.S. corn farmers are paid to produce more corn than people can eat normally. As a result of this overproduction, corn is everywhere. Corn derivatives can be found in nearly one-quarter of all the products in the grocery store—from peanut butter to Twinkies. And of course, corn subsidies led to the creation of a clear, liquid sweetener—HFCS, or high-fructose corn syrup.

Toying with Prices

It isn't only corn subsidies making HFCS as popular as it is today, but also sugar tariffs. While the government reduces the price of corn, it simultaneously hikes the cost of sugar through a complex set of tariffs that make the price of cane and beet sugar more than three times the price of sugar in other nations. Food manufacturers naturally choose the lower-cost corn-based sweetener. Who can blame them?

But this toying around with prices comes with consequences, and *Food Inc.* connects the dots between farm subsidies and America's growing health problems, such as obesity. A report by the Heritage Foundation examined this issue last year [2008] and came to the same conclusion:

What Is High-Fructose Corn Syrup?

High-fructose corn syrup is made by converting the starch in corn to a substance that is about 90 percent fructose, a sugar that is sweeter than the sugar that fuels the body cells, called glucose, and processed differently by the body. The fructose from corn is then mixed with corn syrup, essentially pure glucose, to produce one of two mixtures called high-fructose corn syrup: 55 percent fructose and 45 percent glucose, which is used to sweeten soft drinks, and 42 percent fructose and 58 percent glucose, which is used in products like breads, jams and yogurt.

Jane E. Brody, New York Times,
February 10, 2009.

There is a growing scientific consensus that HFCS likely contributes to the obesity and diabetes epidemics in America, both major contributors to the overall degradation of health in the U.S. The body metabolizes HFCS differently than cane- and beet-based sugars, leading to lower insulin production and an increase in triglyceride fats in the bloodstream. Because of the lower cost associated with foods containing HFCS and hydrogenated soy-based oils (also a byproduct of crop subsidies), this trend disproportionately affects low-income families and those trying to feed a family on a budget. While the real price of healthy fruits and vegetables increased by nearly 40 percent between 1985 and 2000, the price of an HFCS-rich soft drink decreased by 23 percent.

Food Inc. suggests how some of this works by focusing on a family of fast-food eaters. We're introduced to them while they sit at the drive-thru, waiting for their order of burgers,

83

fries, and large sodas. It might be obvious, and perhaps staged, but it gives a real-life example of one reason why people choose to eat unhealthy fast food and HFCS-laden snack foods and sodas—it's cheaper to eat bad food. The family agrees that they should eat healthier, but they find the price of whole and natural foods, such as fresh vegetables, to be too high. The mother says she's very worried about her children, one of whom is on the verge of developing diabetes—no doubt due to bad eating habits.

Chuck the Subsidies

So what's the solution? This is where *Food Inc.* fails miserably.

At the end of the movie, as the screen goes black, ten "simple things you can do" flash on the screen. Among them: Buy organic, shop local and at farmers' markets, and tell Congress that food safety is important to you. These are just adorable, little suggestions for most of the foodie [food enthusiast] types watching the movie. But what about those who can't afford the farmers' market vegetables?

How about suggesting the purchase of inexpensive fresh vegetables like carrots, cabbage, and celery? There are workable and achievable ways people can live and eat healthier. It's simply insulting to suggest to people who have multiple jobs and very little income that they should purchase the highest-priced produce.

And where was the suggestion to tell Congress to chuck farm subsidies? Why wasn't that on the list of ten things you can do?

On the bright side, this movie may encourage two very different groups—right-leaning think-tanks and politicians, and left-leaning environmental and food-watchdog groups—to come together in the cause of ending harmful farm subsidies.

It even ties in with the topic du jour—the future of America's health-care system. Farm subsidies shouldn't just offend economist types who want the free market to dictate prices. They should offend anyone who cares about Americans' health, which should be just about everyone. Ultimately, this may be a more compelling argument to abolish the policy than straight economics.

> *"Assigning all or even some of the blame [for obesity] to farm legislation is a vast over-simplification."*

American Farm Subsidies Are Not to Blame for Obesity

Jim Langcuster

In the following viewpoint, Jim Langcuster contends that America's farm subsidies are not to blame for the nation's obesity problem. Subsidies encourage the growth of crops that are used for both healthy and unhealthy foods, he maintains. Moreover, Langcuster argues, the cause of obesity lies not in types of crops grown by farmers but in the food choices made by consumers. Americans rely on foods made from processed corn because they lack sufficient education about nutrition or adequate money to purchase healthier foods, the author concludes. Langcuster is a communications specialist at Auburn University in Alabama.

As you read, consider the following questions:

1. How much does the government spend to subsidize corn, soybeans, and wheat, according to Langcuster?

2. How does the author respond to the argument that the school lunch program feeds unhealthy food to the nation's children?

3. What example does Langcuster give of a subsidized crop that is used to produce healthy foods?

Does current U.S. farm policy deserve part of the blame for the nation's spiking obesity rates?

Some of the nation's leading public intellectuals apparently think so.

Writing in the April 22 [2007] edition of the *New York Times Magazine*, Michael Pollan contends the current farm bill's heavy emphasis on supporting commodities such as wheat, corn and soybeans is a major contributor to ballooning levels of obesity.

The heavy emphasis on these commodities, Pollan maintains, has begotten a diet rich in all of the ingredients that are making Americans, particularly poor Americans, heavier. He cites an Archie Bunker [an overweight conservative character from the 1970s sitcom *All in the Family*] favorite—Twinkies—as one of the more notorious examples.

"Like most processed foods," Pollan writes, "the Twinkie is basically a clever arrangement of carbohydrates and fat teased out of corn, soybeans and wheat—three of the five commodity crops that the farm bill supports, to the tune of some $25 billion a year."

A Bonanza of Cheap Ingredients?

In fact, he contends, current farm legislation actually promotes the over-production of these commodities, providing a bonanza of cheap ingredients for food processors.

The end result, Pollan maintains, is "a food system awash with added sugars (derived from corn) and added fats (derived mainly from soy), as well as dirt-cheap meat and milk (derived from both)."

Corn Syrup Does Not Cause Obesity

The American Medical Association said in June of [2008] that "high fructose corn syrup [HFCS] does not appear to contribute to obesity more than other caloric sweeteners," and the Food and Drug Administration has affirmed that HFCS is a natural product.

Nebraska Corn Board,
"Web Sites Are Good Resources for the Facts on High Fructose
Corn Syrup," October 23, 2008. www.nebraskacorn.org.

Why, he asks, can't more of these subsidies go for producing healthier foods, namely fresh fruits and vegetables? Equally bad, he says, is that the current farm bill determines the kinds of school lunches our children eat. Indeed, Pollan blames the U.S. Department of Agriculture [USDA] for turning the nation's children into human disposals for the immense overproduction of high-calorie, high-fat foods encouraged by the current farm bill.

If this isn't bad enough, Pollan blames the current farm bill for driving down the cost of several staple commodities worldwide and, in the process, many developing world farmers out of business.

What's needed, Pollan contends, is a farm bill written in the interest of eaters—"people like you and me, increasingly concerned, if not restive, about the quality of food on offer in America."

An Over-Simplified Argument

What's wrong with this picture? Quite a lot, says James Novak, an Alabama Cooperative Extension System economist and Auburn University professor of agricultural economics.

For one thing, the argument is vastly over-simplified, Novak says.

For starters, farm legislation encompasses more than simply paying farmers to produce or not to produce crops, he says, adding that the food stamp program is the largest single spending component of the farm bill.

Moreover, Novak says, the nutrition and commodity components of the farm bill are entirely distinct. Simply put, there is not some ulterior motive by the Department of Agriculture to turn U.S. children into human disposals. Food stamp and school lunch provisions outlined in the farm bill were put there with the sole intention of providing meals to hungry Americans, children in particular, he says.

"The fact remains there still are hungry children in America," Novak says. "Programs to provide breakfasts and lunches to children who might not get them at home aren't a bad thing, in my opinion."

"Likewise, food stamps provide much needed nutrition for the poor."

Indeed, Novak says, the problem isn't so much in the food provided through these programs as it is in the kinds of food choices we make.

On a couple of points, Novak agrees with Pollan. Not enough is being done to educate Americans, particularly limited income Americans, about healthy food choices, he says. Likewise, more money should be provided for poor people to buy healthier foods.

Subsidizing Healthy Food

Nevertheless, Novak says that before fingering USDA as a primary culprit behind ballooning obesity rates, Pollan should remember that many USDA-supported commodities also are used to make healthy food.

Soybeans are a prime example, he says—used to make tofu, soy burgers and soy milk.

Aside from that, Novak says, Pollan is wrong to imply that the planting of more corn and soybeans was hatched in some shadowy corporate boardroom. Indeed, it is the growing desire among producers to capitalize on bioenergy, rather than some shady corporate plot, that led to this year's vast corn and soybean plantings.

Is current farm policy perfect? Absolutely not, Novak says. Even so, he says assigning all or even some of the blame to farm legislation is a vast over-simplification.

Should we be eating more healthily? Absolutely, he says.

"But it's the desire for convenience, processing and the need to cram into our bodies concentrated calories to continue the pace of our hectic lives that figures most prominently into the problem," Novak says.

That, he believes, is a challenge better left to the nation's nutrition and health educators, who deserve more funding from the Nutrition, Research and Education titles of the farm bill, he says.

Periodical Bibliography

The following articles have been selected to supplement the diverse views presented in this chapter.

Sharon Begley	"Born to Be Big," *Newsweek*, September 21, 2009.
Jane E. Brody	"America's Diet: Too Sweet by the Spoonful," *New York Times*, February 10, 2009.
Beth Daley	"Is Plastic Making Us Fat?" *Boston Globe*, January 14, 2008.
Theresa A. Hastert et al.	"Low-Income Adolescents Face More Barriers to Healthy Weight," *Health Policy Research Brief*, December 2008.
Olivia Judson	"Honey, I Plumped the Kids," *New York Times*, August 10, 2008.
Elizabeth Kolbert	"XXXL," *New Yorker*, July 20, 2009.
Steve Rushin	"How Friends Make You Fat," *Time*, August 13, 2007.
Bryan Walsh	"It's Not Just Genetics," *Time*, June 23, 2008.
George F. Will	"Where the Obesity Grows," *Washington Post*, March 8, 2009.
David Zinczenko	"Fight Obesity by Taxing Calories," *USA Today*, October 14, 2009.

OPPOSING
VIEWPOINTS®
SERIES

CHAPTER 3

Who Should Take Responsibility for Obesity?

Chapter Preface

The rise in obesity in recent years has led to a debate over who should bear responsibility for the problem. Some contend the government must address the issue by taking actions that will persuade people to eat better and exercise more, such as taxing fatty foods and building more parks. Others argue that doctors must do more to help their patients make the right lifestyle choices. Still others maintain that schools should remove unhealthy foods and drinks from their premises and do a better job of instructing students about the benefits of nutrition and physical fitness.

In addition to government, doctors, and schools, many commentators insist that parents play a crucial role in preventing obesity in their children. In fact, the role a mother plays may begin before conception. Research has shown that women who lose weight prior to becoming pregnant are less likely to have obese children. And the mother's role continues after conception—pregnant women who eat healthily are more likely to have children who will accept healthy food. As explained by pediatrician Jimmy Unger, "We know that the tastes of the foods Mom eats end up in amniotic fluid. . . . If you want your child to eat fruits and vegetables, then you should start exposing her during pregnancy, and if you don't want the child to crave Twinkies and fries, then avoid them during pregnancy."

Doctors also say that mothers should breast-feed their child whenever possible. Babies who are breast-fed develop into children who are less finicky eaters and are more adaptable to new foods, such as vegetables. "In addition to providing a cocktail of healthy nutrients, breast-feeding may help infants develop a more adventurous palate than formula-fed babies," report Claudia Kalb and Karen Springen of *Newsweek* magazine.

Once their child advances to solid food, parents continue to play an important role in preventing obesity. Experts recommend stocking the house with healthy foods, limiting children's intake of soda, snacks, and fast food, serving nutritious meals, and controlling the size of portions. Surprisingly, doctors do not recommend banning junk foods because doing so causes children to crave them. Instead, parents should allow snacks and sodas as occasional treats. And parents themselves should eat right to model a healthy lifestyle for their children.

In addition to monitoring children's food intake, parents should also encourage their kids to get plenty of exercise. This may mean limiting the amount of time they spend watching TV or playing video games. As with their eating habits, it is important for parents to serve as role models for an active lifestyle. As Kalb and Springen put it, "When parents are sedentary, kids grow up thinking that's the norm."

While parents cannot singlehandedly solve the obesity problem, they play a crucial role along with doctors, government officials, schools, and obese individuals themselves. The viewpoints in the following chapter debate who should take the lead in addressing this major health issue.

| "Why are so many doctors skittish about discussing obesity with its sufferers?"

Doctors Should Take Responsibility for Obesity

Jeremy Brown

In the following viewpoint, Jeremy Brown describes his experience as an emergency room physician who has been hesitant in the past to discuss the problem of obesity with his patients. He concludes that it is essential for doctors to confront the problem of obesity by having frank conversations with their overweight and obese patients. Brown is an associate professor of emergency medicine and the research director in the Department of Emergency Medicine at George Washington University Hospital in Washington, D.C.

As you read, consider the following questions:

1. What sensitive topics other than obesity has the author broached with his patients?

2. What is the appropriate treatment for an obese patient with nontraumatic knee pain, according to Brown?

3. For what conditions did the Society for Academic Emergency Medicine recommend routine screening, as reported by the author?

I have been doing the unthinkable, and the word is out. I am an emergency physician in Washington, [D.C.,] and I've started talking to my patients about their weight.

It has taken me a while to pluck up the courage to speak frankly with obese patients about this problem. For 15 years, I have broached virtually every delicate subject—from sexual histories to the cough that is really cancer—in the noisy, impersonal setting of a busy ER [emergency room]. It is expected of me. It is my job.

So why has it been so hard to talk about this? With an epidemic of obesity in the United States, why are so many doctors skittish about discussing obesity with its sufferers? The truth is, I don't know.

A Wrong Approach

On a recent shift, I treated a woman in her mid-40s who had had pain in her left knee for a month. She had not twisted or injured it in any way that she could recall. There were no signs of infection above the knee. She wanted an X-ray.

She also weighed close to 300 pounds. That's a lot of stress on a joint. Her knees simply cannot keep supporting her weight.

Until recently, I would have ordered an X-ray. Ordering an X-ray makes everyone happy: The hospital charges for taking it. The radiologist charges to read it. The patient often wants the test and is happy to have more than a three-minute evaluation. Once the film is developed, I mention something about there being no fracture and seeing some changes consistent with early arthritis. Then I prescribe some pain relief. The patient would leave feeling vindicated. The problem was captured on film, and the interminable wait was somehow worth it.

Pushing Overweight Patients to Try Harder

I just cannot conceive of a session with an overweight patient that does not involve a discussion of being careful at holiday meals, controlling portion size, avoiding bedtime snacks and trying to exercise three times a week. Somehow it still seems to me that part of a doctor's job is to push patients to try harder.

Barron H. Lerner,
New York Times, July 10, 2007.

Ultimately, though, this approach is wrong. When the emergency room is crowded, it is easy to let the preventive aspects of medicine slip away. Obesity is not only about health risks, which include diabetes, joint pain, congestive heart failure, strokes, back pain, sleep apnea, depression, infertility and erectile dysfunction. It is also about the root causes and our society's denial of the woeful impact that obesity is having on Americans' health.

Let me "not fail to see what is visible" is the line I recall from the Prayer for Physicians attributed to the great physician-philosopher of the Middle Ages, Moses Maimonides, a copy of which hangs over my desk. Nontraumatic knee pain in an obese patient is a sign that she needs dietary counseling, not radiographic imaging.

Prevention Is Part of the Job

Although preventive medicine is not really part of our job description, it has not been ignored by emergency physicians. More than seven years ago, the Society for Academic Emergency Medicine directed its Public Health and Education Task

Force to develop recommendations for prevention that included screenings and counseling.

Possible interventions included pneumococcal immunization [pneumonia vaccination] for seniors, pap screening for women and pediatric immunizations in children. Task force members considered screening for sexually transmitted diseases, tobacco and alcohol use, diabetes, hypertension, HIV and domestic violence. They wondered if we should ask all patients about the safe storage of their firearms and use of smoke detectors.

After reviewing 17 possible interventions, the task force recommended routine screening for alcohol, smoking, HIV and hypertension, immunizations and the referral of children without primary care physicians to a continuing source of care. The next time you cut your finger and go to the ER needing sutures, I should speak to you about these conditions.

Have you noticed what is missing?

There are many opinions about what one can say to overweight patients needing long-term treatment. There is, of course, much that we do not know about obesity. Is it a lifestyle choice, a physical or mental illness or the result of some genetic trait? Should those who are severely obese exercise, follow a strict diet, take anti-obesity medications, undergo surgery or all of the above? If it is confusing to me, it must be harder for my patients. That is why we need to begin this conversation in medical school and continue it through residency and beyond. We need to prepare physicians for this necessary conversation.

> *"Pediatricians would love to be able to solve the obesity problem. But we're also busy addressing literally 299 other public health issues."*

Doctors Cannot Take Full Responsibility for Obesity

Victoria McEvoy

In the following viewpoint, Victoria McEvoy argues that it is unrealistic to expect doctors to solve the problem of childhood obesity on their own. Since obesity is caused by many factors involving parents, communities, schools, and restaurants, society as a whole must pull together to address the issue, McEvoy concludes. McEvoy is chief of pediatrics at the Massachusetts General West Medical Group and an assistant professor at Harvard Medical School.

As you read, consider the following questions:

1. What problems can overzealous antiobesity efforts cause, according to the author?

2. Why is it difficult to address obesity head-on with patients, in McEvoy's opinion?

Victoria McEvoy, M.D., "Doctors Alone Can't Solve Kids' Weight Problems," *Boston Globe*, January 14, 2008. Reproduced by permission of the author.

3. What did the recent University of Michigan poll reveal about parents' beliefs regarding obesity in their children, according to the author?

Two toddlers graced my exam room last month—fraternal twins, one screaming nonstop for the duration of the visit, the other looking around pleasantly, throwing a winsome grin to anyone making eye contact.

Both ate the same foods and kept to the same schedule. But the weight of the protester was considerably less than the mellow sibling's. Did you know that crying burns calories? (Good tip to keep on file.) The twins showcase the important role that personality and metabolism play in body type.

The news shouts to us every day: American children are fat and getting fatter. By some estimates 25 to 30 percent of American children have excess body weight, and there has been a 2.3- to 3.3-fold increase in childhood obesity over the last 25 years.

As panic over these trends escalates, we need to make sure our time and effort spent fighting the epidemic are not wasted. Weight is a very complex issue, and overzealous efforts to control it can lead to eating disorders, self-image problems, and ultimately, ineffective results.

Increasingly, pediatricians are being asked to solve this problem, and while they play an important role in identifying weight issues in their small patients, the solution needs to involve everyone.

Children watch too much television and play too many video games. Streets are unsafe. Parents are too busy for family dinners and are gaining weight themselves. Restaurants supersize portions. Schools cut back on recess. The heavier a child gets, the less likely he or she is to participate in sports, exacerbating the vicious cycle of more eating and less exercise.

A Collective Responsibility

Our children are our future; let's help make their future healthy through efforts to prevent overweight and obesity. . . .

As parents, caregivers, teachers, mentors, public health leaders, and other concerned citizens, it is our responsibility to take immediate action to mitigate this serious and growing public health epidemic. We can and must work collaboratively, using available science and evidence of effective programs to ensure that our children receive encouragement and guidance to make healthful choices for physical activity and good nutrition.

Steven K. Galson,
Bariatric Nursing and Surgical Patient Care,
September 2008.

Misguided Efforts

One misguided attempt to curtail this pattern is to measure pediatricians' performance in managing overweight children. One quality measure recently proposed by insurers was to have each overweight child sent to a nutritionist. The pediatrician would receive a passing grade only if the visit actually took place; the referral alone was inadequate.

Another proposed "quality" measurement for pediatricians would be documented weight loss in an overweight child. Coming next: your friendly pediatrician making house visits to see if you have Twinkies in your cupboard.

Pediatricians would love to be able to solve the obesity problem. But we're also busy addressing literally 299 other public health issues from seat belts to sunblock use. And there's little evidence that what we do—counseling heavy children to eat better and exercise more—is actually effective.

While understanding nutrients is an important part of a general education, research has not demonstrated that sending children to nutritionists leads to weight loss. Any weight-conscious adult understands that just knowing that a carrot has fewer calories than a brownie is hardly the road to sustained, lifelong good health. Similarly, simply telling a child to get an hour of active exercise a day is unlikely to stick.

A Tricky Problem

Pediatricians are told to address obesity straight on with parents. But that's tricky—we mostly see parents when their children are in the exam room, and a pointed comment about being "fat" or "chubby" can lay the groundwork for a later eating disorder or crisis in self-image.

A recent uncomfortable exchange with a mother of three adorable girls I care for highlights the rocky shoals of weight discussions. All three girls were adorable and slightly chubby, but it was obvious that their mom did not want the girls to hear of weight concerns. At each visit we discussed healthy foods, exercise, and their growth charts.

One of the girls had seen one of my colleagues on a weekend, and the doctor had brought up the weight issue quite directly. The mom was furious, although the doctor was doing exactly what the pediatric pundits suggested.

It's helpful when a parent will contact me in advance of an appointment to discuss concerns about body weight, which some do. But a parent in denial about a child's weight problem won't call.

A startling new poll from the University of Michigan's C.S. Mott Children's Hospital revealed that of 2,000 children ages 6 to 11, 25 percent were found to be overweight or obese. But only 13 percent of the parents described their child as having a weight problem.

The rise of childhood obesity is real and serious. Future problems in overweight youth include high blood pressure, increased cholesterol, insulin resistance leading to Type II diabetes, bone and joint problems, disordered sleep, depression, social alienation, and early sexual maturation.

Pediatricians are trying to reverse the trend, but every citizen has a role to play in this epidemic.

| "Much of the obesity controversy is about responsibility. The responsible person is the one eating the food."

Individuals Should Take Responsibility for Obesity

Harold Brown

In the following viewpoint, Harold Brown argues that obese individuals must take responsibility for their condition. Too much of the blame for obesity has been cast on fast-food companies, schools, and grocery stores, he contends. He adds that the government has been too quick to relieve people of their personal responsibility by claiming that the cause of obesity is complicated when in fact it is simple: When people take in more calories than they use, they get fat. Brown is a professor emeritus at the University of Georgia and an adjunct scholar with the Georgia Policy Foundation.

As you read, consider the following questions:

1. How does Brown respond to the Food and Drug Administration's claim that obesity has no single cause?

Harold Brown, "The Cure for What Ails Us: Common-Sense Tactics Are Still Best Way to Get Obesity in Check," *Atlanta Journal-Constitution*, March 10, 2008. Republished with permission of Atlanta Journal-Constitution, conveyed through Copyright Clearance Center, Inc.

2. What laws are being considered in Mississippi and Georgia to address obesity, according to the author?

3. What should be the government's role in solving the obesity problem, in Brown's opinion?

Our culture makes the simplest problems complex and the simplest solutions expensive. None seem simpler than the cause of obesity and its cure, but nutritionists, psychologists, government and popular culture have made its cure both a complex science and mystical mission.

What we learned from nutrition courses a half-century or more ago still holds true today: If we consume more calories than we need, the excess energy is stored as fat. Popular science, however, won't have it. A study group reporting to the U.S. Food and Drug [Administration] says, "The problem of obesity has no single cause." In a nitpicking sense, that is correct. Potatoes, peanuts, hamburgers, ice cream and cake are all causes, as are watching TV, sleeping on the sofa and sitting in front of the computer. Carpentry and running are not.

Many American mothers cajoled their picky children to eat up by reminding them of "the starving children in China." They believed more was healthier. Most of us don't need coaxing now, and China and nearly every other country face their own problems with obesity.

Complicating the Issue

Simply leaving this up to the individual to solve has become too complicated. Even the World Health Organization noted in a recommendation to help combat European obesity, "Holding individuals alone accountable for their obesity should not be acceptable." Hence hundreds of how-to books, legions of nutritionists and dozens of government agencies to solve the problem.

Mississippi legislation would prohibit restaurants from serving to those the state defines as obese. Georgia's getting in

A Matter of Personal Responsibility

Is it government's role to help us reduce our rolls? Or is it a matter of personal responsibility? . . .

People make choices. And government should protect—not restrict—the freedom to make those choices so long as we're not harming others.

While we may not always like the choices others might make, it is essential that we all have the freedom to choose for ourselves.

Sally C. Pipes, Washington Post, *December 26, 2007.*

on the game, with a bill that would have public schools weigh children periodically to keep a running check on obesity. How that data will be used is unclear, but the intent is to enlist schools in the war on obesity. Interestingly, poverty and hunger was a main reason for the National School Lunch Program. Is the program working too well? Poverty has changed over the years; many now believe it causes obesity.

If schools are to become an action agency in matters other than education, will they now become both the encourager and restrainer in nutrition?

Reassigning Blame

Much of the obesity controversy is about responsibility. The responsible person is the one eating the food, unless they are too young or too enfeebled to understand. But the net is being cast wide to reassign responsibility and designate perpetrators. The blame goes to McDonald's and other fast food places, and school cafeterias, grocery stores, ice creameries and even soft-drink companies, all accused of conniving to, or at least condoning, fattening the public. TV is to blame; if not for the laziness it induces, then for advertising fattening foods and lifestyles.

It is no wonder that Americans overeat. We're encouraged by food commercials, food channels and strategically placed items on overflowing supermarket shelves. There's extra time to eat the food we don't have to grow, harvest or slaughter, much less prepare. Technology has so reduced the physical exercise and time required to produce or earn our food that we have to look for ways to expend more energy and eat less. But even the least educated know that improvement in food and its production is a good thing.

And they know how to solve the obesity problem.

Information Readily Available

So why does the government need to be so involved? Because big government has never seen a personal problem that it didn't think it owned. The Surgeon General's Call to Action to Prevent and Decrease Overweight and Obesity 2001 suggested that governments "create and promote policies that promote an environment in which healthy dietary and physical activity options are readily accessible."

The kind of advice needed is already on the National Institutes of Health Web site as simple [daily calorie intake] guidelines to attain or maintain your weight:

- > 10 calories per pound of desirable body weight if you are sedentary or very obese;

- > 13 calories per pound of desirable body weight if your activity level is low, or if you are over age 55;

- > 15 calories per pound of desirable body weight if you regularly do moderate activity;

- > 18 calories per pound of desirable body weight if you regularly do strenuous activity.

Calorie content is listed on nearly every package of food sold. It is readily available for those foods that are not packaged. All that's necessary, however, is to read the bathroom scales every few days and adjust food consumption or exercise accordingly.

A Personal Problem

Belittling the growing obesity problem and its health consequences doesn't help. But the cost of the planning and enforcement required to solve this problem is outrageous. So is the money individuals spend on dietary foods, weight-loss remedies and advice. Overweight individuals ought to be free to spend their money on anything they think helpful, whether foolish or faddish. It's a personal problem, to be solved or tolerated by those persons.

Government involvement should be limited to education and advice, and it doesn't take dozens of agencies and legislative acts to provide it. Slim Jims or Jeans shouldn't have to pay the government to reinvent the wheel for this simple lifestyle equation: Fat equals calories eaten minus calories used.

| *"While some form of nutrition educa-
tion is offered in many schools, it's very
limited because the government doesn't
see it as a priority."*

Schools Should Take Responsibility for Obesity

Adam Bornstein

*In the following viewpoint, Adam Bornstein argues that schools
need to do more to combat obesity. Although many schools are
trying to provide healthy food, he contends, many are forced by
economic necessity to offer unhealthy items in their cafeterias
and to permit soda vending machines in their hallways. The federal government must provide more funding to ensure that
schools serve healthy food and deliver adequate nutrition education, Bornstein concludes. Bornstein is the fitness editor for
Men's Health magazine.*

As you read, consider the following questions:

1. What loopholes in the National School Lunch Program
   allow the selling of unhealthy foods at schools, according to the author?

Adam Bornstein, "Why Are Schools Selling Junk Food to Our Kids?" *Men's Health*, vol.
23, November 2008, p. 158. Copyright © 2008 Rodale, Inc. Reproduced by permission.

2. Why do schools sell "competitive foods," according to Bornstein?

3. How has the No Child Left Behind Act affected nutrition education, in the author's opinion?

It's no secret that childhood obesity is a major problem in America's schools. What's so baffling, though, is that despite our awareness, it's a growing problem. After all, one solution seems obvious and simple: Pull the plug on vending machines, ban junk food on campuses, and serve only healthy fare in cafeterias. Case closed, right? If only it were that easy.

"The government system is forcing our schools to choose," says Katie Wilson, Ph.D., president of the School Nutrition Association, a nonprofit organization dedicated to improving school meals and nutrition. "Schools can either provide only healthy foods and go into debt, or allow unhealthy options, which generate revenue but are also a contributing factor to weight gain."

This unappetizing proposition, says Wilson, is the result of education budget cuts and a flawed system. But while it may be hard to swallow, it's just one piece of the puzzle. That's because, well, french fries taste good. So do candy bars, potato chips, and soda. "Unless kids are properly educated, they're going to choose junk over healthy food at school and at home," says Wilson. "Unfortunately, the number one question children ask me about nutrition is, 'Why don't schools teach us right from wrong?'"

We wondered that, too. We also wanted to know how, exactly, a system meant to help kids is ultimately making them fat.

The School Lunch Program

As odd as it sounds, one of the key contributors to poor nutrition in schools—at least indirectly—may be the National School Lunch Program (NSLP). Established in 1946, this federally subsidized program provides calorie-balanced meals at cost to all children, or at reduced or no cost to children in low-income families. The intention, of course, is to give every child access to an inexpensive, healthy lunch. And to ensure that this goal is met, the U.S. Department of Agriculture (USDA) has set these basic nutrition standards for schools to follow.

All meals must provide one-third of the Recommended Dietary Allowance (RDA) for calories, protein, vitamin A, vitamin C, iron, and calcium. This makes sense, considering that children consume 19 percent to 50 percent of their daily calories in the school cafeteria, according to the USDA.

The meals must also match the USDA's Dietary Guidelines for Americans, which limit the fat content of a meal to 30 percent of total calories and cap saturated fat at less than 10 percent.

The program forbids foods of "minimum nutritional value" from being served inside the school cafeteria at mealtimes. These are items that provide less than 5 percent of eight specific nutrients—i.e., "empty-calorie" foods such as gum, soda, and jelly beans, which are primarily sugar.

All of which sounds sensible, but plenty of loopholes exist, particularly in that last requirement: Turns out, foods of minimum nutritional value, while not allowed for sale in the cafeteria, can be sold anywhere else in the school—for instance, from a vending machine on the way to the lunchroom. What's more, candy bars, chips, and doughnuts actually avoid the foods-of-minimum-value designation. (A main ingredient in many of these foods is refined flour, which by federal law is fortified with vitamins and minerals.) As a result, they can be sold in the lunchroom, side by side with healthier options. Of course, that's only if the schools choose to do so. And that leads to the bigger issue: dollars and cents.

Schools in a Financial Bind

"Schools lose money every day because it costs more money to prepare meals than the reimbursement they get from the federal government," says Donald Schumacher, M.D., medical director for the Center for Nutrition and Preventive Medicine, in Charlotte, North Carolina. Case in point: In 2008, the government increased the NSLP subsidy to schools, to $2.57 per meal per student, but the cost to prepare the lunches rose to $2.88. And while schools that purchase foods directly from the USDA receive an additional 20 cents per meal, they're still at an 11-cent deficit.

That amount might seem trivial, but multiply it by the 29.6 million children participating in the NSLP and it comes out to a daily nationwide deficit of $3.2 million. For perspective, a middle school with 1,000 students would be $19,800 in the hole after just 1 year.

Schools can raise prices, of course, and some are being forced to do so. But Wilson says this strategy leads to other problems: It defeats the purpose of providing low-cost, healthy meals in the first place, and it can also result in fewer kids purchasing the nutritionally balanced lunches.

Competitive Foods

The upshot is that schools have instead turned to offering "competitive foods." These items aren't part of the NSLP. They include foods of minimal nutrition—which can be sold in vending machines, school stores, and snack bars—as well as foods that don't meet other USDA guidelines but that can be offered a la carte in the cafeteria. This is where the trouble really begins. For instance, students buy competitive foods in greater proportions than the USDA-approved meals, taking away from their consumption of fruits and vegetables, according to a report to Congress presented by the Center for Science in the Public Interest [a nonprofit public interest advocacy organization]. So while the NSLP helps schools serve healthy food, it has also opened the door to options that undermine that effort.

"Without full funding from the government, schools are being pinched, and we need a quick way to make money," says Wilson. "That's why we have vending machines. That's why we sell a la carte. And that's why we purchase unhealthy foods along with healthy foods. They're cheaper than the healthier foods, and we can turn a greater profit."

A (Partial) Success Story

With 71 schools and 64,000 students, Volusia County, Florida, is one of the largest school districts in the country. And when it comes to instituting nutrition reform, it's also one of the most progressive. "Schools have a responsibility to address healthy eating and fitness," says district superintendent Margaret Smith. "And we're determined to protect the health of our students."

So despite a crisis that has forced the closing of several schools, Smith's district has instituted policies to ensure that fresh fruit, vegetables, and whole grains are offered in all schools on a regular basis. At the elementary level, signs are placed throughout cafeterias encouraging students to make healthy food choices, and water is placed at eye level in vending machines to compete with sports drinks. Soda is permitted only in high schools and only after the lunch hour is over. And this year, one school in the district, Pierson Elementary, was among 43 schools nationally recognized for their promotion of healthy initiatives.

But Volusia administrators openly admit that the problems haven't been eliminated entirely. For example, some high-school students still have easy access to vending machines throughout the buildings after lunch is over. "Vending machines provide revenue that helps fund extracurricular activities for students," says Joan Young, the school district's director of cafeteria services. This is one way the district manages to keep athletic programs afloat in the midst of big budget cuts.

And while healthy dishes are readily available in Volusia schools, the cafeteria also stocks what many teenagers would consider more desirable options, including chocolate cake, cookies, and pizza.

Rising Prices

But remember, Volusia is working hard to fix these flaws. Many school districts across the country aren't so proactive. And all of these issues are compounded by the soaring cost of food due to high oil prices and a weak dollar. "I've been working in the food industry for 30 years and I've never seen price increases like the ones we've experienced over the past 18 months [2007–2008]," says Bob Bloomer, regional vice president of Chartwells-Thompson, a subsidy of Compass Group, the largest food distributor in the world.

Even small price fluctuations can have a major impact: A five-cent increase in the price of milk will cost the Volusia school district an additional $750,000 in the 2008–2009 school year. And Young has especially noticed price increases for the so-called healthiest items, such as whole-wheat bread and products with less sugar.

"The minute you say 'healthy,' it costs more," says Bloomer. "When you say 'zero trans fat,' it costs more. It's the nature of the beast." In Albany County School District 1 in Laramie, Wyoming, margarine with no trans fat costs 262 percent more than the option with trans fat, leading the schools to use the less healthy version. "There are some districts that just don't have the money. They don't care about whole wheat. They don't care about trans fat. And when I say they don't care, I mean they just can't afford it," says Bloomer.

In the end, superintendents and the school board are left with a dilemma: Find new ways to raise millions of dollars, or buy the types of foods students will purchase. "School administrators know that foods of minimum nutritional value provide a profit margin that makes up for what they're losing from the federally mandated meal," says Dr. Schumacher. "And these products can even give them a little bit of profit to put back into the school. Where is their incentive to stop that?"

National Reform Needed

Make no mistake: Many schools are trying, according to the School Nutrition Association. In fact, 71 percent of them have attempted to make a "significant" effort to offer healthy food choices on their menus. And several states now ban vending machines in elementary schools or limit what can be sold in the machines and when students can access them. But clearly, it's going to take sweeping national reform to repair this problem.

New legislation is a good place to start, says Dr. Schumacher. He's working hard to push a bill, HR 1363, that will hopefully help build momentum for improving children's nutrition in schools nationwide. The proposal is an update to the Child Nutrition Act of 1966. It uses current nutrition science to rewrite the definition of foods of minimum nutritional value and requires that they be removed from schools, effectively eliminating a multitude of unhealthy options. "The issue isn't about removing children's ability to make choices, it's about providing healthy options and making it harder for them to access bad foods," says Dr. Schumacher. [HR 1363 did not pass and become law.]

Research has shown that this strategy, along with education, can help. In a Temple University study of grades four through six, researchers removed all sodas, sweetened drinks, and snacks that didn't meet USDA nutrition standards from vending machines and cafeteria lines in five Philadelphia schools. They also implemented 50 hours of nutrition education for students and encouraged parents to purchase healthy snacks for their kids to eat at home. After 2 years, half as many of these kids became overweight, compared with kids in similar schools without the program.

Education Is Our Fat Burner

While those numbers are encouraging, they also underscore the daunting challenge of overcoming childhood obesity. Sure, the study results sound impressive. But some of that is nifty data-crunching—7.5 percent of the children in the prevention program packed on too many pounds, compared with 15 percent of the group that made no changes. Still, we have to start somewhere. And there's little doubt that a combination of approaches is necessary. "If you don't teach kids what's good and what's bad, you don't solve a whole lot by restricting things," says Wilson. "Education is our fat burner."

One barrier is the No Child Left Behind Act. Designed to improve the quality of education in public schools, it puts tremendous pressure on schools to ensure that students perform well on standardized tests in math and science. But as a result, physical education and health classes have been minimized—crippled, even—since tests aren't given in those subject areas.

So while some form of nutrition education is offered in many schools, it's very limited because the government doesn't see it as a priority.

"Until more money for federally funded school food programs and a mandate for nutrition education are in place, we'll always be in this situation," says Wilson. "We need a major support from our national government."

The Smoking Precedent

Interestingly, there may be a parallel between today's childhood obesity epidemic and the youth smoking problem from the 1970s, says Marlene Schwartz, Ph.D., the director of research and school programs for the Rudd Center for Food Policy and Obesity at Yale University. Back then, Schwartz recalls, no one thought the situation would improve. But as education matched preventive measures, children became informed and behaviors changed.

A 2007 University of Michigan study found that only 22 percent of high-school seniors said they had smoked a cigarette in the previous 30 days, compared to 1976 when the number was 39 percent.

The big changes didn't begin, though, until the mid-1990s, when the government began to make it more difficult for the tobacco industry to target America's youth, according to the report.

Dr. Schumacher has seen the impact of this type of childrens' nutrition education in the research he's conducted. "Recently, one of our children went home for dinner and saw his father pouring ketchup all over his food," recalls Dr. Schumacher. "This fourth-grade kid took the bottle and said, 'Dad, you need to read this label. Look how much sugar you just put on that.' And I thought, Wow."

Children answering health questions rather than asking them? Maybe that's the true solution to the obesity epidemic.

Periodical Bibliography

The following articles have been selected to supplement the diverse views presented in this chapter.

Greg Cebrzynksi   "Responsibility of Parents Has Been Forgotten in Furor over Ads' Effect on Childhood Obesity," *Nation's Restaurant News*, January 8, 2007.

Ellen Goodman   "Putting Obesity Out of Business," *Boston Globe*, July 24, 2009.

Arun Gupta   "Gonzo Gastronomy: How the Food Industry Has Made Bacon a Weapon of Mass Destruction," AlterNet, July 23, 2009. www.alternet.org.

Theresa A. Hastert et al.   "Teen Dietary Habits Related to Those of Parents," *Health Policy Research Brief*, December 2009.

Derrick Z. Jackson   "The Big, Fat Truth About Americans," *Boston Globe*, August 1, 2009.

Perri Klass   "When Weight Is the Issue, Doctors Struggle Too," *New York Times*, July 21, 2009.

Sally C. Pipes   "Brave New Diet," *Washington Post*, December 26, 2007.

Steen Stender, Jørn Dyerberg, and Arne Astrup   "Fast Food: Unfriendly and Unhealthy," *International Journal of Obesity*, June 2007.

Jacob Sullum   "Fat Load," *Reason*, August 5, 2009.

Jimmy Unger   "Parents' Role in Obesity Starts Early," *Eugene (OR) Register-Guard*, July 15, 2007.

OPPOSING
VIEWPOINTS®
SERIES

CHAPTER 4

How Can Obesity Be Reduced?

Chapter Preface

Attempts to reduce obesity include efforts by both individuals and the government. At the individual level, weight-loss methods include diets, exercise, medications, and gastric-bypass surgery. At the government level, officials propose added taxes on sugary drinks, increased regulations on junk-food advertising, and zoning laws that encourage the development of communities with lots of bike paths and parks.

One government proposal that has provoked controversy in recent years is the idea of requiring fast-food restaurants to post the calorie counts of their meals on their menu boards. Several localities already have menu-labeling laws in effect, including New York City; Westchester County, New York; and Kings County, Washington. Others have passed or are considering such laws, including California; Philadelphia, Pennsylvania; and Davidson County, Tennessee. Proponents insist that menu-labeling laws are necessary in order to inform customers who otherwise would have no idea how fattening some food choices are. The Center for Science in the Public Interest (CSPI), a nonprofit organization that works to educate the public about food-safety issues, explains the rationale behind menu-labeling laws:

> Without clear, easy-to-use nutrition information at the point of ordering, it's difficult to make informed choices at restaurants. Few people would guess that a small milkshake has more calories than a Big Mac or that a tuna sandwich from a typical deli contains twice as many calories as the roast beef with mustard. Armed with this information, the CSPI argues, customers can make wise choices that could ultimately lead to less obesity.

Opponents of labeling laws contend that such laws will do little to solve the obesity problem. Some critics point out that calorie-count labels have been required on supermarket foods for years, but they have not prevented an increase in obesity. As expressed by Steve Chapman, a columnist for the *Chicago Tribune*, "The federal government first required packaged foods to carry such information in the mid-1970s, and today, we are collectively fatter than we were then. . . . Either people don't notice what's in the food they buy, or they don't let the knowledge affect what goes in their mouths." Chapman concludes that menu labels will not impact people's meal choices because "they prefer to eat whatever they like."

Menu labels are just one solution proposed to reduce the obesity problem. Additional solutions, including soda taxes and food advertising restrictions, are debated in the following chapter.

| *"The formula for staying slim is simple: Calories in, calories out."*

Dieting and Exercise Can Help People Lose Weight

Anne Moore

In the following viewpoint, Chicago journalist Anne Moore argues that while many factors contribute to obesity, the main cause is eating too much and being too inactive. Therefore, the best way to lose weight is to eat smaller portions, choose healthier foods, and get more exercise. Moore writes that she lost 10 percent of her body weight and two dress sizes by making changes in her eating and exercising habits. She encourages other overweight and obese people to follow her example.

As you read, consider the following questions:

1. How much money is spent on obesity-related health care costs, according to Moore?

2. According to the author, how many pounds of pressure is put on the knees for every pound a person is overweight?

3. What event nudged the author to start losing weight?

Fat consumes 10 percent of our health-care dollars. That's $147 billion we spend, as a nation, treating diseases caused or exacerbated by too much fat on our frames.

We spend even more—50 percent—on aging. But aging is natural. We fight it, we deny it, we postpone it. Still, all of us age and die: It's worth shelling out for a comfortable end.

Fat, on the other hand, is a preventable expense.

So for a nation roiled by the cost of expanding health care, a soothing solution presents itself: If we slim down, we'll need less care, we'll spend less money, avoid disease, and maybe even save our lives.

Fat Wreaks Havoc

Know what happens to your body when it's weighed down by fat? After it settles in the usual places, like your hips or your butt or your arms or your gut, fat invades and settles in your organs. Havoc ensues. Hearts get too big, arteries clog, organs falter and then fail. Diabetes, stroke, heart attack, heart failure, some cancers: all caused by or linked to fat.

"We're not set up to store excess fat in a harmless way," says Dr. Robert Kushner, a professor of medicine and director of clinical programs at the Comprehensive Center on Obesity at Northwestern University.

Fat kills. And before it kills, fat makes you miserable. For every pound overweight, three pounds of pressure falls on your knees. Ten pounds overweight? That's—ouch!—30 pounds of pressure. Twenty, that's 60. Fat puts pressure on your hips and lower back too. Joints become arthritic. "Pass the potatoes" becomes "Pass the ibuprofen [pain reliever]."

Ignore the fat advocates [who say it is natural and harmless to be fat]: This stuff is deadly. And it costs all of us: Half of that $147 billion is paid by Medicaid and Medicare, funded by Social Security taxes. Disease and disability, prescription drugs, heavy-duty hospital beds, extra-wide wheelchairs, bari-

Physical Activity Guidelines for Children, Adolescents, and Adults

Children and adolescents should do 60 minutes (1 hour) or more of physical activity daily. . . .

It is important to encourage young people to participate in physical activities that are appropriate for their age, that are enjoyable, and that offer variety.

All adults should avoid inactivity. Some physical activity is better than none, and adults who participate in any amount of physical activity gain some health benefits.

For substantial health benefits, adults should do at least 150 minutes (2 hours and 30 minutes) a week of moderate-intensity, or 75 minutes (1 hour and 15 minutes) a week of vigorous-intensity aerobic physical activity, or an equivalent combination of moderate- and vigorous-intensity aerobic activity. Aerobic activity should be performed in episodes of at least 10 minutes, and preferably, it should be spread throughout the week.

U.S. Department of Health and Human Services, 2008 Physical Activity Guidelines for Americans," October 2008.

atric lifts [machines for moving obese people], extra-wide cuffs to measure blood pressure: That's the cost of fat.

If we get the fat off and out of our bodies, we can get the fat out of spending.

The Cause of Obesity

How did we get so fat? Two-thirds of Americans are overweight or obese. Thirty years ago obesity was a blip, at 15 percent of the population. We're among the world's most educated people, and the formula for staying slim is simple: Calories in, calories out.

If we're so smart, why are we so fat?

Throw a dart, you'll hit a reason: fast food, skinny models, towns without sidewalks, excess wealth, urban poverty, working women, farm subsidies, sugared cereals, school lunches, high-fructose corn syrup, deep-fried candy, television, the Internet, desks.

Did my desk make me fat? Sitting too long at it played a part. But it's not my desk's fault I put on weight. It's mine, it's yours, it's ours. We got off the scale and turned a blind eye to the kinds and amount of food we put in our bodies.

We became a fat nation. Race, age, income, sex, geography; fat does not discriminate.

Should government fix our fat? Employers? Insurers? Should our sodas and bags of chips and candy bars be taxed?

I don't think so. We made ourselves fat, one by one, and we can make ourselves slim again, one by one. After all, we became a nation of savers again [during the recession of 2007–2009].

Last summer in New York, my sister turned to me and said, "What happened? You were always so slender."

My sister has the looks and manner of the actress Amy Adams in [the movie] "Enchanted." Everything that comes out of my sister's mouth sounds kind. Hers was a statement of fact, delivered sweetly: I was fat.

Changing Diet and Exercise

When I got home to Chicago I resolved to become the slender person I used to be. How? I like to eat, and I cook for a family of five; a diet wouldn't work. A lifelong swimmer, I already exercise more than most people. I needed a plan I could live with forever.

Smaller portions, no seconds, more fruit, less bread and cheese, longer walks. (I hate running.) A friend's trainer told me to swim faster; I swapped sprints for laps.

I started losing weight right away.

It's been a year; I've lost 10 percent of my body weight and two dress sizes. Friends and acquaintances stop me all the time: "You're so slender!"

Would I have changed if my sister hadn't said anything? Maybe what we all need is a gentle nudge.

Dana Joy Altman, 44, is a slender beauty whose expertise is culled from daily living. She writes about food and markets and cooking on her Real Food Rehab blog. (Preparing meals at home is a key to weight management, studies show.) With beautiful graphics, and humor, Altman steers readers to affordable, quality ingredients. Those who need a push instead of a nudge hire her for a "pantry makeover" that includes shopping and cooking instruction. Chicagoan Leslie Bodenstein, 45 and lean, rearranges her own busy schedule to take friends and acquaintances to a Bikram yoga class. She's not a teacher; she wants others to experience a practice that results in well-being. So when she hears someone complaining about fatigue or poor skin or weight gain, she pipes up. She nudges gently, she says, but sometimes resorts to text messages. "Everyone has their excuses, but you've got to start."

To fix our health-care system, we have to fix ourselves.

So get to it: Declare yourself the "Biggest Loser" on your block, in your town, in your city. Dance your butt, your thighs, your back, your belly off. Join a friend for a walk, a swim, a bike ride. Cut your meals in half. Skip seconds. Spread the word: Fat kills.

Borrow my sister's sweet tone and turn to someone you love: "What happened? You were always so slender."

> "Permanent, substantial weight loss appears to be almost impossible by diet and exercise alone."

Dieting and Exercise Are Largely Ineffective

Judy Foreman

In the following viewpoint, Judy Foreman argues that attempts to lose weight by means of diet and exercise are futile for most overweight and obese people. Once people become overweight or obese, she writes, hormones that control appetite make sure the body hangs on to the excess fat. For this reason, when overweight people lose weight, they usually gain it back. Foreman suggests that people who are overweight or obese should try to eat healthily and exercise in order to remain as fit as possible despite their extra pounds. Foreman is a health columnist for the Boston Globe.

As you read, consider the following questions:

1. What percentage of obese people can lose weight through diet and exercise, according to Dr. Lee Kaplan, as cited by the author?

2. What is the body's "set point," as defined by Foreman?

Judy Foreman, "Let the Post-diet Era Begin," *Boston Globe*, October 1, 2007. Reproduced by permission of the author.

3. Why does the author believe that genes are not to blame for today's obesity problem?

Is permanent, significant weight loss really possible?

If you're talking merely 10 to 20 pounds—and nobody knows the actual figure—you probably can diet and exercise your way to a svelter self and stay there, provided you stick with your weight control program rigorously. Forever.

But if you're among the two-thirds of adult Americans who are overweight or obese, permanent, substantial weight loss appears to be almost impossible by diet and exercise alone.

Only about 1 to 2 percent of obese people can permanently lose weight through diet and exercise alone, said Dr. Lee Kaplan director of the weight center at Massachusetts General Hospital.

"Dieting is like holding your breath," he said. "You can do it, but not for long. Your body is stronger than your willpower."

In other words, Americans have probably wasted way too much time, money, and hope on diet programs that don't help enough. It still makes sense, however, to eat as healthily as you can and to do whatever you can to avoid gaining any more weight.

The Ineffectiveness of Dieting

One famous study conducted at the University of Minnesota during World War II illustrates the ineffectiveness of severe dieting. The researchers put 36 physically and emotionally healthy young men of normal weight on a strict diet, allowing them only half the calories they were used to. The men lost weight, but became psychological wrecks, obsessing about food, bingeing, and, even after the diet was over, eating way too much, often 8,000 to 10,000 calories a day until they regained the weight, recounted *New York Times* science writer Gina Kolata in her recent book, *Re-thinking Thin.*

In another classic study in the 1950s, researchers at Rockefeller University in New York City recruited obese people who were so desperate to lose weight that they agreed to live in the hospital for eight months, including a four-month period in which they subsisted on only 600 calories a day of liquid formula. They lost weight, Kolata noted. But, to the dismay of subjects and researchers, they all quickly regained the weight.

The Role of Hormones

That's because the basic biochemistry of the body's weight management system can work against even highly motivated dieters.

When a very fat person loses a lot of weight by diet and exercise, the brain goes into panic mode, reading a complex array of chemical signals as proof of impending starvation. Metabolism slows. The body hangs on to every calorie it can get. The chemical signals that trigger appetite soar, creating a drive to eat so powerful you can't resist. From the standpoint of evolution, this makes sense: Our DNA was built when we were hunter-gatherers to protect us against starvation, not obesity.

Consider one of the best-studied weight control hormones, leptin, which is made in fat cells and is designed to tell the brain: "Stop eating. I'm full."

"Obese people usually have high levels of leptin because they have so many fat cells making it," said Dr. Eleftheria Maratos-Flier, an obesity researcher and associate professor of medicine at [Boston's] Beth Israel Deaconess Medical Center. "The heavier you are, the higher the circulating leptin." In theory, being fat should mean that the brain would be flooded with "stop eating" signals.

Exercise Is Useless for Weight Loss

The conventional wisdom that exercise is essential for shedding pounds is actually fairly new. As recently as the 1960s, doctors routinely advised against rigorous exercise, particularly for older adults who could injure themselves. Today doctors encourage even their oldest patients to exercise. . . . But the past few years of obesity research show that the role of exercise in weight loss has been wildly overstated.

"In general, for weight loss, exercise is pretty useless," says Eric Ravussin, chair in diabetes and metabolism at Louisiana State University and a prominent exercise researcher. Many recent studies have found that exercise isn't as important in helping people lose weight as you hear so regularly in gym advertisements or on shows like *The Biggest Loser*. . . .

The basic problem is that while it's true that exercise burns calories and that you must burn calories to lose weight, exercise has another effect: it can stimulate hunger. That causes us to eat more, which in turn can negate the weight-loss benefits we just accrued. Exercise, in other words, isn't necessarily helping us lose weight. It may even be making it harder.

John Cloud, Time, August 9, 2009.

But when people go on severe diets, "they lose more leptin than you would expect. So the brain thinks there is less fat than there ought to be," which makes people eat more, she said.

And leptin is just one of many hormones involved in weight control. "In the stomach and intestines alone," Kaplan said, "there are 36 hormones that regulate weight, and another

30 in the brain. The end result of all these chemicals is to keep our energy stores, that is, fat, in balance."

The Body's "Set Point"

Put differently, some researchers believe that one reason weight loss programs ultimately fail is that diet and exercise do not change the body's "set point," the thermostat-like mechanism in the hypothalamus and other parts of the brain that keep weight fairly constant.

Dr. David Heber, director of the University of California, Los Angeles (UCLA) Center for Human Nutrition, is more optimistic about the effectiveness of dieting. "The set point can be changed. Yes, there are signals to eat and to hoard fat, but having said that, humans do adapt to starvation and do change," he said. While the hormones that control appetite and satiety do tilt the equation toward regaining lost weight, "psychology trumps physiology. I see people every day who have overcome their genes and kept their excess weight off for decades."

Many researchers do agree that one weight loss strategy does seem to change the set point—bariatric surgery, the stomach-stapling procedure. Doctors used to think it worked by simply reducing the size of the stomach, preventing people from eating much. Now, they think it works because, with less stomach tissue pumping out hormones such as ghrelin, which stimulates appetite, a person's appetite and satiety signals may be altered to help them eat less.

A Liberating Message?

So if dieting sets up a battle between our free will and our hormones, are America's fat masses wasting their time desperately trying to lose weight?

To some, including the National Association to Advance Fat Acceptance, a civil rights organization that is fighting discrimination against fat people, all this suggests not so much a hopeless message as a liberating one. "Most people do not choose to be fat," said the group spokeswoman, Peggy Howell. "But once people are fat, it is next to impossible to change that. It's far healthier to accept who you are and get on with your life than to be obsessed with what goes into your mouth."

That makes a lot of sense to me, though I resist the idea that our genes are the big culprits because we have basically the same genes today that our skinnier grandparents had. What's changed is our lifestyles—more sitting around eating Twinkies, less walking to and from daily activities.

So, here's my take. Because of the body's complex biochemistry, it's very difficult to lose weight once you gain it. So, exercise as much as you can—for general health, in addition to weight control. Eat right—fewer refined carbs, more fruits and veggies—again, for general health. If you're fat, don't just blame your genes and let yourself get fatter and fatter.

At the same time, be gentle with yourself, and with fat people you see.

> "A week after my [gastric bypass] surgery, I'd lost 11 pounds. A month after, I'd lost 30 pounds. Less than two months later, I bought a size 16—down from a 22!"

Gastric Bypass Surgery Can Help People Lose Weight

Cassie Pisano, as told to Cristina Gonzalez

Gastric bypass surgery, also known as bariatric surgery, is a procedure in which the stomach is surgically shrunk in order to reduce the body's intake of food, resulting in weight loss. In the following viewpoint, Cassie Pisano, a graduate student who lost one hundred pounds after undergoing gastric bypass surgery, describes her experience to Redbook *writer Cristina Gonzalez. She recalls how she was teased in high school and felt extremely self-conscious about her weight in college. Believing her obesity was preventing her from living a normal life, she decided that gastric bypass surgery was her only option—a decision she does not regret.*

Cassie Pisano, "Gastric Bypass Surgery Gave Me My Life Back," *Redbook*, vol. 211, September 2008, pp. 110, 112, 115. Copyright © 2008 Hearst Communications. Reproduced by permission of the author.

As you read, consider the following questions:

1. How much does Pisano say she weighed by her senior year in college?

2. What does the author say she does when she gets "head hunger"?

3. What is Pisano's incentive to keep from regaining the weight she lost?

"I Had More Fun as the School Mascot than as a Cheerleader"

I used to love being a cheerleader in high school—until my senior year, when I quit the team. I was tired of kids yelling nasty comments at me during cheer routines because of my weight, which fluctuated between 170 and 200 pounds, and it was embarrassing to have to special-order a size 18 uniform. I became the school mascot instead, and hiding in the lion costume was such a relief after all the public ridicule. I constantly measured myself against other people, and though I don't remember asking them to, my friends did the same: They would tell me who I was fatter than and who I wasn't as big as. They made me feel so self-conscious; even when I was just hanging out with them, I felt anxious and isolated. I had never been an overeater as a child, but now food was my only comfort. It totally owned me: I'd eat freely, then feel guilty after, and gain more weight. Every once in a while, I'd try to diet, but the scale never moved.

"I Failed a Class Because I Was Too Self-Conscious to Go"

When I got to college, I felt like every girl there was a size 2. Just being in school while obese was hard: I failed a class because I was too self-conscious even to go. I played trumpet in the school band, and when we flew to away games, I was mortified to see my hips oozing over onto the seat next to me. I tried Weight Watchers, the South Beach Diet, the cabbage soup diet, diet pills, everything. I'd lose maybe 5 pounds—a drop in the bucket.

By the time I was 20, I had developed an eating disorder. For two years, I ate only half of a bagel or a PowerBar a day and made it down to a size 14. I stopped after a guy I was dating sat me down and convinced me I was being dumb. Then he slept with my roommate. Again, I turned to food for comfort. By senior year, I was 250 pounds—the biggest I had ever been.

"Living Your Dream Is Scary"

After graduation, I got my first job, and shared an office with someone who'd had gastric bypass surgery. When I met her, I thought, She's beautiful. I could never look like her. But then she told me her story. So I went to an information session where a surgeon explained the three types of weight-loss surgery. Afterward, I felt optimistic. If this worked, I wouldn't ever have to worry about fitting into a seat. I could finally have a normal life.

Next, I was checked out by a cardiologist [heart doctor], a pulmonologist [lung doctor], and a psychiatrist; I also went to nutrition seminars. This gave me time to decide if surgery was what I really wanted. I still wasn't sure. I started a journal of things I hated about being fat—like those looks at the gym that said, "Why are you here?" Finally, I decided surgery was the only way to lose a significant amount of weight and keep it off. I chose gastric bypass because with other procedures (like stomach stapling or lap band) I'd still be able to eat sugary, high-fat foods with no consequences. I needed to make a bigger change. But I was scared. I scheduled the appointment, then felt like I was going to throw up. I'd always wanted to be skinny, but to dream it is one thing. To live it is different.

Gastric Bypass Before Pregnancy

An overweight woman who has weight-loss surgery before becoming pregnant may help break the cycle of obesity in her family. . . .

Researchers found that children born to women who had weight-loss surgery before pregnancy have improved heart health and a lower risk of obesity compared with their siblings who were born before the mother had surgery.

Shari Roan, Los Angeles Times, *September 7, 2009.*

I had my surgery on April 11, 2006. I took some pictures at home, said good-bye to the old me, and walked out the door. Once I got to the hospital, everything happened so fast. The surgery took about two hours. My surgeon stapled across the top of my stomach, creating a small pouch the size of a golf ball. Then he sewed part of my small intestine directly into the pouch. This would redirect food to bypass most of my stomach and enter my small intestine instead. I was in the hospital for two days. When I woke up, I felt like I had done 200 sit-ups, but that was the worst of the pain. Over the next three months, I went from a liquid-only diet to soft food to regular food. I was frustrated at first, but excited and anxious to see results. I thought, I can do this.

"I'm in Charge Now"

A week after my surgery, I'd lost 11 pounds. A month after, I'd lost 30 pounds. Less than two months later, I bought a size 16—down from a 22! Was that really me in the mirror? For the first time, when people told me I was beautiful, I believed it.

Today, I'm in charge. I used to be a slave to my appetite, but my life no longer revolves around my next meal. I never feel physically hungry anymore—which is so freeing! It offends me when people say surgery is the easy way out. This certainly isn't easy. I still fight emotional eating; I get that "head hunger" when I'm bored or stressed. When that happens, I try to focus on my family and friends, scrapbooking, or going to the gym. And I know what the consequences would be if I were to eat a meal as big as the ones I was used to: an entire frozen pizza, or a burger, fries, and a soda. The surgery rerouted food away from the part of the intestine that helps me digest sugar and carbs, so if I eat too much of them, I go through "dumping"—my body tries to get rid of what I just ate. I get sweaty and light-headed. And if I overeat anything, it comes back up.

"I'm a Completely Different Person"

I used to get dirty looks when I went out. Now people offer me drinks! I love the attention—I just eat it up. My weight had always made it too difficult to play sports. But today, I'm a hiker, a skier, and I'm training for a triathlon. I have everything I ever wanted, thanks to surgery, and I'm so grateful. I have respect for my body. I'm getting my MBA [master of business administration degree] and I have a wonderful boyfriend. I want to be healthy, to have a family, and to be a good role model for them. That's enough incentive for me to keep off the 100 pounds I lost. I keep my size 22s handy to remind myself of how far I've come.

"*Twenty-two percent of bariatric-surgery patients experienced complications before they even left the hospital.*"

Gastric Bypass Surgery Can Be Dangerous and Ineffective

Sabrina Rubin Erdely

Gastric bypass, or bariatric, surgery is a medical procedure in which the size of the patient's stomach is reduced in order to limit the amount of calories the body is able to take in. In the following viewpoint, Sabrina Rubin Erdely argues that the operation, which is increasingly performed on obese people, often results in unpleasant or even tragic complications. In addition, she writes, while many bariatric surgery patients lose a large amount of weight, they often gain much of it back. Erdely is a journalist, feature writer, and contributing editor for Self *magazine.*

As you read, consider the following questions:

1. How many bariatric surgeries were performed in 2007, according to Erdely?

2. What percentage of bariatric-surgery patients have complications before leaving the hospital, according to the research cited by the author?

3. What is "dumping syndrome," as described by Erdely?

E ileen Wells was smiling as she was wheeled into surgery. She was too excited to feel nervous. At 38, she was about to get "a new lease on life," she says, echoing jargon in weight loss surgery ads. She had seen the before and after pictures in celebrity tabloids, watched the TV infomercials, listened to the patient testimonials and researched online. She was ready to begin her own transformation. At 5 foot 3 and 290 pounds, she was sick of being fat. Her joints ached. Her feet hurt. A stroll through the mall near her home in Greenwood Lake, New York, was enough to leave her sweat-slick and gasping for air. She was anxious to say good-bye to sleep apnea and dieting, ready to take control. And so in March 2005, Wells underwent a laparoscopic [done through a slim tube using fiber optics, which needs only a very small incision] gastric bypass. She was grinning right up until the anesthesia knocked her out.

From the menu of weight loss (bariatric) operations, Wells had chosen the Roux-en-Y bypass, the most popular option in the United States. The surgery sectioned off her stomach to a thumb-sized sac—sharply limiting the amount of food Wells could eat—then connected it to a deeper portion of her small intestine, to limit absorption of the calories she did consume. (An increasingly popular alternative, gastric banding, cinches in the stomach to restrict its capacity.) The rearrangement required Wells to radically overhaul her eating habits. She learned to eat tiny, frequent meals, cutting her food into pencil eraser-sized bites. On her doctor's orders, to replace nutrients no longer absorbed by her digestive tract, she faithfully swallowed a multivitamin, calcium and B12 supplements and two protein shakes daily. Soon she resembled the women in those weight loss infomercials: Fifteen months post-op, Wells had lost an amazing 160 pounds—more than half her body weight—bringing her down to a trim 130.

No Guarantee of Success

But although Wells looked like a satisfied customer, she didn't feel like one. Seven months after surgery she had developed an agonizing ulcer on the new inner seam between her stomach and intestine, which required a second operation. Not long afterward, Wells recalls eating a bite of tuna steak her husband, Ron, had prepared and doubling over in pain; an ambulance rushed her into surgery yet again, this time for an intestinal hernia—her bowel had snagged on a slit in her abdominal wall. A fourth procedure followed to ease the pain of the abdominal scarring from her previous surgeries. Meanwhile, Wells's gastrointestinal pain had become so severe that she could barely eat. One day while shoe shopping, she realized she couldn't flex her right foot. Within weeks her limbs began to tingle, her energy evaporated and her weight plummeted. She stopped menstruating. By late 2006, Wells had shrunk to 105 pounds.

"I feel like I'm dying," she told Ron. Months of doctors' visits revealed that Wells had beriberi, a disorder caused by extreme thiamine deficiency. Rarely seen outside 19th-century Asia, it's present enough among those in the weight loss-surgery world that doctors call it bariatric beriberi.

"I was a model patient! I did everything right!" Wells says today, still in disbelief that after all the hype and hope, her surgery turned out so disastrously. But as she learned the hard way, doing everything right after bariatric surgery is no guarantee of success.

Miracle Cure?

That fact may come as a surprise: With glowing media reports of its health benefits and a roster of celebrity success stories, weight loss surgery is beginning to feel like the miracle cure of the moment. Last year [2007], doctors performed 205,000 bariatric surgeries, marking an 800 percent increase from a decade ago. As of 2004, 82 percent of patients are women, according to the U.S. Agency for Healthcare Research and Quality (AHRQ) in Rockville, Maryland. Weight loss surgeries are poised to become even more popular in the wake of findings that gastric bypass and banding can send type 2 diabetes into remission in many people. A 2007 report from the University of Utah School of Medicine in Salt Lake City found that obese patients who had bypass surgery had a 40 percent reduced risk of dying in the seven years after the procedure, compared with obese people who didn't have the surgery. Bariatric surgeons are using results like those to make the case for surgery as a preventive measure against cancer, heart disease and diabetes in patients who are severely obese.

But despite the growing popularity of obesity surgery—and the general perception that it's a shortcut to thinness and good health—it's no easy path. The American Society for Metabolic & Bariatric Surgery (ASMBS) in Gainesville, Florida, puts gastric-bypass surgery's death rate at between 1 in 1,000 and 1 in 200. In one AHRQ study, 4 in 10 patients developed complications within the first six months, including vomiting, diarrhea, infections, hernias and respiratory failure. Up to 40 percent of gastric-bypass patients can suffer nutritional deficiency, potentially resulting in anemia and osteoporosis [a bone disease]; seizures and paralysis have been reported in extreme cases. Some of these malnourished patients experience bizarre neurological problems, as Wells did.

An Uncertain Proposition

Even if patients avoid the major pitfalls, they could be in for a world of intestinal discomfort. Not to mention how difficult it is to retrain yourself to subsist on 3-ounce meals and vitamin pills after surgery. "If you're here for the quick fix, then this surgery is not for you," affirms Kelvin Higa, M.D., immediate past president of ASMBS. "This is a serious lifelong commitment." It's an adjustment so profound that patients are screened to make sure they're psychologically up to the task—a test that, according to a recent study in the *Journal of Clinical Psychiatry*, one fifth of would-be patients fail.

All this for a surgery that the experts admit is poorly understood. Few randomized, controlled studies (the gold standard of research) have been performed comparing gastric bypass with nonsurgical weight loss therapy. Although initial weight loss can be dramatic—gastric-bypass patients typically shed around 70 percent of excess weight—patients gradually regain 20 to 25 percent of what they lose. For people with extreme obesity, defined as having a body-mass index of 40 or greater, gastric bypass often merely shifts them into the obese category. Obese patients can drop to overweight status (a BMI of 25 to 29.9). Yet fewer than 10 percent of patients achieve a normal BMI of 18.5 to 24.9, reports Lee Kaplan, M.D., director of the Massachusetts General Hospital Weight Center in Boston. Altogether, weight loss surgery remains an uncertain proposition, and although potential patients must meet certain criteria . . . , experts caution that the surgery is definitely not meant for the mainstream. "Because it's risky, it's only appropriate for a tiny fraction of people with obesity—the sickest 1 to 2 percent," Dr. Kaplan says. "The idea that all obese people should get surgery is insane." Yet that's the way weight loss surgery is being peddled to the public. . . .

The Unadvertised Complications

Operating on the obese always presents major challenges. "One of the first tenets you're taught as a surgical trainee is to fear fat," Dr. [Neil] Hutcher says, in part because it crowds the organs and makes it hard to see. Twenty-two percent of bariatric-surgery patients experienced complications before they even left the hospital, findings in the journal *Medical Care* reveal. Those problems ranged from the life-threatening—such as infection and respiratory failure—to milder complications such as vomiting and diarrhea. And a 2005 *Journal of the American Medical Association* study found that 20 percent of gastric-bypass patients were rehospitalized the year after surgery, sometimes for follow-up operations. (Those same patients' hospitalization rate averaged 8 percent in the year before the procedure.) "It's those additional surgeries you worry about, because there's a significantly increased risk in repeat operations," largely due to internal scarring, points out Mass General's Dr. Kaplan.

In September 2006, 37-year-old Jennifer Ahrendt of Jacksonville, Florida, was one year post-op, having shed an astonishing 200 pounds, when she was struck to the floor by a bolt of pain. "It was excruciating, right in the center of my breastbone and straight through to my back," Ahrendt remembers. "It felt like everything inside me had ruptured." A trip to the emergency room revealed Ahrendt had gallstones—a condition shown to strike about 40 percent of gastric-bypass patients—and would need another surgery to remove them. Ironically, gallstones are a sign of weight loss success, because rapid weight loss crystallizes cholesterol in the gallbladder, forming hard deposits. They are so common that many bariatric surgeons remove the gallbladder during the initial surgery. After all, bypass surgery makes that organ irrelevant: Its job is to store bile, whose destination—the first portion of the small intestine—has been wiped off the anatomical map.

Bowel Obstructions

Gallbladder flare-ups are the least of a patient's post-op worries. Bowel obstructions, a risk in any surgery, are an especially serious danger for those who have gastric bypass. "What you have then is a blind loop: The intestine is obstructed in one direction and partitioned in the other direction, so there's no exit," Dr. Higa explains. "If they don't get surgery within 12 hours, the bowel could dilate and explode," potentially killing them.

A Better Solution for Obesity

A growing number of obese teens—not to mention their parents—are looking to surgery to help them shed the pounds that threaten their health. . . .

A much better way to deal with juvenile obesity is to take action before it gets out of hand. And the best way to do that is through a two-pronged approach: Eat properly and get plenty of exercise.

Reading (PA) Eagle, June 19, 2007.

Tammy Cormier of Mamou, Louisiana, found that out the hard way. In October 2003, doctors diagnosed a bowel obstruction after Cormier developed the worst pain of her life. "It was worse than childbirth," she remembers. Doctors knocked her out and wheeled her into surgery to resolve the problem. But a month later, Cormier was out to dinner with friends when she again cried out in stomach-clutching agony. In the hospital, tests revealed another bowel obstruction. The last thing she remembers is being rushed into surgery. She woke up three days later in intensive care, hooked up to a ventilator. Cormier recalls, "It was traumatic, one of the most horrible experiences of my life," leaving emotional scars so deep that recently, while on a Caribbean cruise for her honeymoon, a cramp in her side brought on a full-blown panic attack. "All I could think about was ending up back on that ventilator," she says.

GI Disasters

Because gastric bypass rearranges the digestive tract, it's unsurprising that patients can find themselves rife with gastrointestinal (GI) complaints. Eighty-five percent of people who have gastric bypass experience "dumping syndrome," when sugary, undigested foods empty directly into the small intestine, causing nausea, light-headedness, cramping and gas. And then there are the true GI disasters, such as the horror Dana Boulware went through. Almost immediately after her [gastric] banding procedure in January 2003, Boulware started having trouble keeping food down.

"It was like surgically induced bulimia," says Boulware, a 46-year-old data entry specialist in Houston. "No matter how small a bite I took, no matter how much I chewed, I would feel it just sitting there—a pain in my chest like a heart attack. Then it would come right up." She managed to tough it out for 20 months because, she says, her surgeon urged her to stick with it, continually telling her to chew her food more thoroughly. Finally, when Boulware's esophagus felt scarred from vomiting and the enamel had worn off her teeth, a second surgeon advised removing the band. Boulware readily agreed—"I think I would have taken it out myself if I had known how," she says. Still, she considers herself lucky. Boulware's best friend had a similarly unhappy gastric-band experience but was determined to give surgery another try. In September 2005, her friend underwent a duodenal switch—a relatively uncommon form of weight loss surgery that involves removing a large portion of the stomach and bypassing a significant section of the small intestine—and developed a leak in her bowel. She died days later of sepsis.

When the Fat Makes Its Way Back

Some bariatric-surgery patients may rationalize any suffering they experience as the cost of losing weight. But even so, they may not keep the pounds off—and the svelte ideal they're aiming for may be a pipe dream in the first place.

Lisa Tannehill of Grants Pass, Oregon, had high expectations when she had a duodenal switch at age 38. "I'm a big believer in the surgery," she avers—and remains so despite having to fight through a post-op nightmare of a hernia and a reaction to pain meds. In the first 18 months, she dropped 100 pounds from her 325-pound frame. From there, however, Tannehill's weight plateaued—and then, to her horror, the pounds began creeping back on. "I didn't do anything differently!" she says. "I still ate tiny meals!" Nevertheless, six years post-op, Tannehill has leveled off at 240 pounds, a net loss of 85 pounds.

The greatest period of weight loss is the 12 to 18 months after bariatric surgery, after which you start to see weight regain, according to Meena Shah, Ph.D., an obesity researcher at the University of Texas Southwestern Medical Center at Dallas. Her 2006 review of the controlled studies done on the issue revealed that the disease-fighting properties of both bypass and banding surgery go down as patients' weight goes back up. . . .

Giving Up on a Miracle

Months of surgeries and nutrition therapy failed to pull Eileen Wells out of her downward spiral. "I was a skeleton, just wasting away," she remembers. "My doctor told me that if I didn't gain weight, I might die." Which is why in June 2007, Wells found herself being wheeled into surgery yet again—crying this time—en route to having her gastric bypass reversed. . . .

For women who wanted so desperately to lose weight, going back to square one feels like the ultimate defeat. "Do I regret having gastric-bypass surgery? Yes, I regret it," Wells admits. She maintains that for some people who are severely overweight, the procedure can be a lifesaver, even though her bypass put her out of work for nine months—and her reversal hasn't totally corrected her neurological symptoms. "I thought I was doing something to change my life for the better. But it made me feel a hundred times worse."

*"The government should take steps to
restrict the current onslaught of food
marketing that targets children."*

Regulating Food
Advertising to Children
Will Reduce Obesity

Susan Linn and Courtney L. Novosat

*In the following viewpoint, Susan Linn and Courtney L. Novosat
argue that the rise in childhood obesity has occurred in tandem
with an increase in marketing of junk food to children. Because
the food industry has failed to self-regulate, the authors contend,
government regulation of food advertising is necessary to reverse
the childhood obesity epidemic. Linn is an instructor in psychiatry at Harvard Medical School. Novosat is the program coordi-
nator at the Campaign for a Commercial-Free Childhood, an
organization that works to reduce advertising and marketing of
products to children.*

Susan Linn and Courtney L. Novosat, "Calories for Sale: Food Marketing to Children in
the Twenty-first Century," *Annals of the American Academy of Political and Social Sci-
ences*, vol. 615, January 2008, pp. 133–34, 147–50. Copyright © 2008 by Annals of the
American Academy of Political and Social Science. Reprinted by permission of SAGE
Publications.

As you read, consider the following questions:

1. How much money do food and beverage companies spend each year on advertising that targets youth, according to the authors?

2. Why did Kellogg's agree to curtail its marketing to children in 2007, as reported by Linn and Novosat?

3. What are two of the suggestions for policy changes presented by the authors?

Childhood obesity is a serious and escalating public health concern, yet children are targeted as never before by marketing for high-calorie, nutritionally deficient foods.

Overweight children are at risk for a number of medical problems, including hypertension [high-blood pressure], asthma, and type 2 diabetes, a disease previously found primarily in adults. Since 1980, the proportion of overweight children ages six to eleven has doubled to 15.3 percent; for adolescents, the rate has tripled to 15.5 percent. The most recent studies suggest that "over 30% of American children are overweight or obese" while "only 2% eat a diet consistent with United States Department of Agriculture (USDA) guidelines" [according to researchers Ameena Batada and Margo G. Wootan]. This unprecedented escalation of childhood obesity mirrors the equally unprecedented escalation of largely unregulated marketing that targets children. In 1983, corporations were spending $100 million on television advertising to children, which was essentially the only avenue available. By 2000, Burger King spent $80 million on advertising to children and Quaker Oats had allocated $15 million just to market Cap'n Crunch cereal. Today, food and beverage advertisers alone spend between $10 billion to $15 billion a year targeting youth. Given the exponential rise in dollars spent on marketing to children, there is little doubt that the food industry believes that marketing is a critical factor in children's food choices—and research bears that out. . . .

Food Marketing at Home and Abroad

The United States currently regulates marketing to children less than most other industrialized democratic nations. Sweden and Norway ban marketing to children younger than twelve. The Canadian Province of Quebec bans marketing to children younger than thirteen. Greece prohibits ads for toys on television between 7 a.m. and 10 p.m., while ads for toy guns and tanks are not allowed at any time. In Flemish-speaking areas of Belgium, no advertising is allowed within five minutes of a children's television program shown on a local station. Finland bans advertisements that are delivered by children or by familiar cartoon characters. The French parliament banned all vending machines in middle and secondary schools. Moreover, advertising regulations proposed by the European Union would ban commercials that imply that children's acceptance by peers is dependent on use of a product, while New Zealand is considering a wholesale ban on junk food marketing to kids. In recent years, Britain has begun to take steps to curb marketing to children. In 2004, the British Broadcasting Corporation severed marketing connections between their children's programming and junk food companies. In addition, a bill in Parliament to ban all junk food marketing on television until after 9:00 p.m. currently has significant support.

In the United States, the escalation of marketing to children and the rise of childhood obesity have occurred while the Children's Advertising Review Unit (CARU)—the advertising industry's self-appointed watchdog—has served as the primary self-regulatory agency responsible for monitoring child-directed advertising. This problematic internal monitoring has led advocates to call for increased government regulation of food marketing to children. However, the current administra-

Percentage of Obese and Overweight U.S. High School Students by Sex

	Obese	Overweight
Female	9.6%	15.1%
Male	16.3%	16.4%
Total	13.0%	15.8%

Percentage of Obese and Overweight U.S. High School Students by Race/Ethnicity

	Obese	Overweight
White	10.8%	14.3%
Black	18.3%	19.0%
Hispanic	16.6%	18.1%
Total	13.0%	15.8%

TAKEN FROM: Centers for Disease Control and Prevention, "Youth Risk Behavioral Surveillance—United States, 2007," *Morbidity and Mortality Weekly Report*, June 6, 2008. www.cdc.gov.

tion [of President George W. Bush] is philosophically opposed to regulation. Corporations are quick to exploit what has become a national zeitgeist [cultural climate] of individual responsibility. The food industry has been a powerful lobby and food marketing to children is a profitable endeavor; it is naïve to think that companies are going to completely stop marketing their products to children without external regulations or that such regulations are going to come about without significant grassroots pressure from advocacy groups.

Lawsuits: An Inefficient Method

In June 2007, for instance, Kellogg's agreed to curtail its marketing to children younger than twelve and to stop marketing using media-licensed characters by 2008—but only as the result of negotiations following the threat of a potential lawsuit. The Campaign for a Commercial-Free Childhood (CCFC), the

Center for Science in the Public Interest (CSPI), and two Massachusetts parents filed an "intent to file suit" in the Commonwealth of Massachusetts Superior Court. . . .

While the extent of Kellogg's agreement to adopt stricter nutrition and marketing standards that reduce sugar and fat in their products, and advertising to children is unprecedented in the food industry, the agreement is still flawed. The negotiated standard for sodium is less stringent than that recommended by the Institute of Medicine (IOM) for foods acceptable in schools, and there is concern that the standard for sugar is too high. More than that, the shortcomings of the agreement underscore an important point: a lawsuit, or the threat of one, is not an efficient way to establish national policy. Addressing the problem on a company-by-company basis drains valuable time and already scarce resources from advocacy groups.

Flawed Pledges

Nevertheless, the formalized threat of a lawsuit heightened awareness and escalated pressure on food companies to curtail their child-targeted marketing. On July 18, 2007, to stave off threats of government regulation, eleven major food companies announced details of their own voluntary pledges to restrict marketing to children and, for the first time, to open their marketing plans to the Better Business Bureau and CARU. How effective these pledges will be in actually restricting junk food marketing to children remains to be seen. Taken as a whole, however, these pledges represent many of the flaws inherent in self-regulation. Companies are not adhering to any uniform standard; rather, each company sets its own standard, which means that monitoring compliance is going to be quite difficult. More problematic, at no point has the entire food industry agreed to restrict marketing to children. As this [viewpoint] is written [2007], Burger King, Nestle, ConAgra, and Chuck E. Cheese have publicly refused to participate. Finally, history suggests that because these pledges are voluntary and not legally binding, they can be broken, sidestepped, or even remain unimplemented with little or no consequence.

In June 2007, a month before the food companies' pledges were released, Representative Edward Markey (D-Mass.) ended a meeting of the House Committee on Energy and Commerce Subcommittee on Telecommunications with a promising warning: "The First Amendment is precious, but children are just as precious. We need a healthy balance to make sure our children aren't bombarded with these messages." He continued, "Most parents are not in the position to control what kids see—they are both working. While these kids have all these unhealthy choices presented to them in the media, if there is not a proper response from industry, I'm prepared to press the Federal Communications Commission (FCC) to put on the books rules to protect kids from unhealthy messages." Markey's warning echoes that of Senator Tom Harkin (D-Iowa), who made a similar comment about the Federal Trade Commission (FTC) at a 2005 workshop on food marketing and self-regulation. He and Senator Sam Brownback (R-Kansas) have formed an advisory committee to work with the FCC on issues of food marketing to children. In addition, as of this writing, the FTC is readying subpoenas to forty-four food companies and fast-food restaurants for a congressionally mandated study on food marketing to children. At this time, it is hard to know what the results of this government activity will be, but these efforts are significant. They occasion the federal government's first movements toward adopting a strong stance to curb marketing unhealthy food to children since 1980, when Congress restricted the FTC's ability to regulate marketing to children.

Self-Regulation Has Failed

The rise of childhood obesity mirrors the unprecedented increase of food marketing aimed at children. Companies bypass parents and target children directly in a myriad of ways through the media, through toys, and even in schools. While food companies and the marketing industry tout self-regulation as a solution to the problem, current levels of child-targeted food marketing and the rise in childhood obesity strongly suggest that self-regulation has failed.

From a public-health perspective, what makes the most sense is to prohibit marketing brands of food to children altogether. When childhood obesity is a major public health problem, certainly there is no moral, ethical, or social justification for marketing low-nutrient, energy-dense foods to children. Even marketing healthier brands to children through media-linked spokes-characters or ads on television and the Web seems problematic. Do we want to encourage our children to make food requests or purchases based on commercials whose marketing implicitly or explicitly suggests a product will enhance their social life, make them happier, or increase their power—messages routinely embedded in advertising?

Government Must Act

We should also question the wisdom of depending on the food and media industries to promote healthy eating to children. The partnership between the producers of [animated movie] *Shrek the Third* and the Department of Health and Human Services is emblematic of the inherent conflict of interest between encouraging healthy lifestyles and promoting the consumption of unhealthy food. It does not seem wise to depend on corporations, bound by law to promote profits, to be the guardians of public health. Instead, on both the state and federal level, the government should take steps to restrict the current onslaught of food marketing that targets children. The reality of drafting and bringing to fruition such legislation is both complex and cumbersome, but that should not prevent a creative and rigorous exploration of a wide range of options for restricting food marketing to children. The following are suggestions for changes in policy that would limit the amount of child-targeted junk food marketing:

- Congress should restore to the FTC its full capacity to regulate marketing to children.

- The marketing and sale of brands associated with unhealthy food products in schools should be prohibited, including corporate-sponsored teaching materials.

- Corporate tax deductions for advertising and marketing junk food to children could be eliminated.

- Product placement of food brands could be discouraged in movies, video and computer games, and television programs popular with children and adolescents by requiring that such embedded advertising be identified when it occurs.

- Food companies should be prohibited from using advertising techniques that exploit children's developmental vulnerabilities, such as commercials that encourage kids to turn to food for empowerment, or to be popular, or for fun.

- The use of licensed media characters to market food products to young children should be prohibited, as should child-targeted sweepstakes and contests.

- We should prohibit links between toy and food companies that lead to food-branded toys and toy giveaways by fast-food companies such as McDonald's and Burger King.

- We should support a truly commercial-free public broadcasting system that would provide programming for children free of any marketing, including brand licensing. It is not in children's best interest to depend on the food industry to be the guardians of public health. Only an across-the-board set of policies—designed and enforced by a body from outside the food and marketing industries—can both protect children's health and maintain a level playing field between companies.

> *"As marketers . . . , we need to . . . refuse to silently accept the blame that some would lay upon us, and to disseminate information about the true causes of the obesity epidemic."*

Regulating Food Advertising to Children Will Not Reduce Obesity

Brady Darvin

In the following viewpoint, Brady Darvin argues that food and beverage advertising is not responsible for the rise in childhood obesity. While advertising influences children's purchase requests and consumption patterns, he concedes, research shows that parents, rather than advertising, are the strongest influence on children's eating and drinking behavior. Therefore, he concludes, proposed government regulations on food and beverage marketing to children are misguided and should be opposed. Darvin is senior director of consumer insights at Strottman International, Inc., an advertising agency that specializes in marketing to children and families.

Brady Darvin, "Don't Play the Blame Game: Efforts to Further Regulate Advertising Candy and Snacks to Kids Poses a Threat to U.S. Marketers," *Confectioner*, vol. 92, September 2007, pp. 68–71. Reproduced by permission.

As you read, consider the following questions:

1. What were the conclusions of the analysis of food advertising published in the June 2007 issue of the *Archives of Pediatrics & Adolescent Medicine*, as reported by the author?

2. According to the Kaiser Family Foundation study Darvin cites, what percentage of parents said food advertising was their biggest concern when it came to the effects of television viewing on their children?

3. Why is it unrealistic to limit children's exposure to food and beverage advertising, in the author's opinion?

It affects one-third of American kids. It is responsible for skyrocketing statistics on the number of new cases of childhood diabetes and heart disease. It is going to be the primary contributor to bringing the U.S. healthcare system to the brink of bankruptcy.

"It," of course, is the current obesity epidemic. If you read or listen to the news headlines like the average American, you might believe that the primary cause of this epidemic is marketing. This definition of marketing includes television advertising for fast food and sugary cereals, Web site games that encourage kids to scarf down cookies and candy, and grocery aisles lined with packages sporting popular cartoon characters.

If you listen to "authorities" such as the Center for Science in the Public Interest (CSPI) or the Campaign for a Commercial Free Childhood, you would believe that today's kids are so inundated with messages encouraging them to eat junk food that they have no hope of making healthier choices. You would believe that the number of such messages today's kids see is higher than it's ever been and has been growing every year. And, if you're a parent of an overweight child, you might even believe that legislation is needed to prevent marketers from "bombarding" your kids with unhealthy messages, and that other countries that have such laws don't have obesity problems.

Of course, if you believe all of the above, you are probably not reading *Confectioner*. But if you're in the business of selling candy or snacks, and if kids are directly or indirectly responsible for some part of your sales, you surely have some customers who do believe all of the preceding, and it's important that as a retailer you know the facts.

Just the Facts

The marketing and advertising of "junk food" is not the cause of the recent rise in childhood obesity. That is not to say, however, that television advertising does not influence children's food and beverage purchase requests and their short-term food consumption patterns. Advertising and promotions work, and that shouldn't be a surprise to anyone.

But the more relevant issue when discussing the increase in childhood obesity is whether the average child between the ages of 6 and 11 has been exposed to more ads for unhealthy foods than children of 10, 20 or 30 years ago.

Not so, according to the most recent analysis on this subject, published in June 2007 in the *Archives of Pediatrics & Adolescent Medicine*. That analysis incorporated a review of the 10 largest studies of kid-targeted food ad exposure over the past 30 years. It concluded that "the dramatic increase in childhood obesity rates during the past few decades was not mirrored by similar changes in food advertising exposure," and that "comparisons with previous studies suggest that, over time, food ads account for a smaller share of the product ads seen by children."

Dissecting the Research

Another study published this past June [2007], this one by the Kaiser Family Foundation [a public policy research organization], surveyed 1,000 parents about their feelings on how television viewing affected their kids. While two-thirds of parents agreed that kids who watch a lot of television are more likely to be overweight, only one-third said they were "very" concerned that their children are exposed to too many television ads, with another 35 percent saying they were "somewhat" concerned. But of those parents who are concerned, only 10 percent cited food advertisements as their biggest concern. (Toys, video games, clothing and alcohol were all of greater concern to these parents.)

In addition, the study found that the vast majority of parents have a lot more influence over their kids than the media does, and only 14 percent of parents listed the media as one of the top two influences in their children's lives. Kids' No. 1 influence, according to parents: Mom and Dad.

A 2005 study by leading youth researcher Yankelovich [Company] found similar sentiments when it asked more than 1,200 parents to assign responsibility for solving kids' health issues. The parents attributed only 10 percent of the responsibility to food manufacturers and marketers, but 49 percent to themselves.

Legislating Change

Despite the research demonstrating that most parents are not blaming advertisers for childhood obesity, legislation that mandates an outright ban on advertising certain foods to kids is a very real threat for American marketers. The U.K.'s [United Kingdom] Ofcom (an agency similar to the Federal Communications Commission [FCC] in the United States) earlier this year announced a ban on television ads for foods high in fat, salt or sugar during programs watched primarily by children. In France, regulators decreed in March 2007 that advertisements for any processed food targeting kids must devote 7 percent of space to health messages about a balanced lifestyle and healthy eating.

A Confectionery Industry Advertising Promise

The confectionery industry is committed to advertising its products within the framework of the overall diet, appropriate energy balance, and eating occasion depicted. To accomplish this goal, confectionery advertising:

- Will feature a reasonable portion size for the situation depicted.

- Will portray the advertised product as a snack, treat, or dessert and not as a substitute for a meal.

National Confectioners Association,
"Advertising Confectionery to Children: Statement of Principles
by the Members of the National Confectioners Association,"
www.candyusa.com.

Marketers in both France and the United Kingdom are currently fighting these bans, which threaten the rights of marketers in a free economy. If you are reading this magazine [*Confectioner*], you should be equally concerned because some U.S. legislators, led by Sen. Tom Harkin, D-Iowa, and Sen. Sam Brownback, R-Kan., are considering similar legislation for our country.

In Norway and Sweden, statutory bans on all ads targeted at kids have been in place for more than a decade. Despite this, the childhood obesity rates in those countries are right in line with the United States.

Banning Ads Not Realistic

Those groups like the CSPI that advocate banning advertising for foods deemed "unhealthy" also seem to ignore the reality that it's simply not possible to limit kids' exposure to ads for foods and beverages without banning all food and beverage advertising to everyone. A large share of television programming and many other types of media seen by kids are actually targeted to adults. (The majority of the 10 most popular programs among kids ages 6 to 11 air during prime time, not on Saturday mornings or during the afternoons.)

To advocate that today's kids must be shielded from all media advertising foods that may be unhealthy is to advocate the elimination of all marketing and advertising for foods and beverages—period. While some extremists might actually like to see that happen, retailers can take comfort in the fact that such a scenario is not a feasible or realistic possibility, in our free economy. However, it is almost certain that marketers and retailers in the United States will be more restricted in their future advertising practices when it comes to kids.

Sens. Brownback and Harkin announced this summer [2007] that they would postpone a report from a task force they formed with the FCC in view of industry plans to announce concessions, but they are still likely to push for more strict legislation in the near future.

Self-Imposed Limits

Less than two weeks later, just before a scheduled Federal Trade Commission hearing to discuss the topic, 11 of the nation's largest food and beverage marketers announced plans to introduce self-imposed limits on advertising targeted to children ages 12 and under. Seven of the companies pledged to avoid the use of licensed characters in print and online, unless they are promoting products that meet certain nutritional guidelines, although they may still use such characters on product packaging without violating those pledges.

Shortly following that announcement by food makers, in just one week last month, Nickelodeon, Cartoon Network, and Discovery Kids—three of the largest licensors of kids' characters and brands—each separately announced similar pledges to end all agreements allowing their characters and brands to be used in conjunction with any foods or beverages that do not meet minimal nutritional guidelines. Each pledge uses slightly different nutritional criteria, and each exempts "special occasion" products, such as Halloween candy.

While all three companies have received kudos from government officials and advocacy groups for the pledge, those groups have made it clear they want to see further restrictions. Rep. Edward Markey, D-Mass., released a statement the same day that Nickelodeon announced its pledge, saying, ". . . I look forward to working with Nickelodeon, as well as with other industry participants, on additional initiatives they can make in the coming weeks and months to further address childhood obesity issues." It seems clear that such extreme critics will not be happy until marketers' rights are legislated away completely.

A Call to Action

The National Confectioners Association [NCA] earlier this year published guidelines for responsible marketing to children. The guidelines encourage marketers to advertise their products appropriately and to present balanced messages that feature reasonable portion sizes and encourage healthy lifestyles. (www.candyusa.org)

Now more than ever, it's critically important to embrace these guidelines. At the same, time, however, as marketers, retailers and manufacturers of candy and snack foods, we need to pull together, to refuse to silently accept the blame that some would lay upon us, and to disseminate information about the true causes of the obesity epidemic. We need to be active in the fight against legislation that would restrict the advertising and promotion of our products.

Contact the NCA and ask how you can help with this cause; educate yourself about childhood obesity, portion control, and how to encourage healthy habits in your customers. Follow the same advice being given to today's kids: Don't just sit around: Get active.

| "Losing weight is never easy, but one of the most effective diets would start with a soft drink tax."

Taxing Sugary Drinks Will Reduce Obesity

Nicholas D. Kristof

In recent years, some policy makers have proposed adding an extra tax on sugary beverages such as soft drinks and energy drinks. Advocates contend that such a tax would reduce consumption of unhealthy beverages similar to the way cigarette taxes are credited for lowering smoking rates. In the following viewpoint, Nicholas D. Kristof, a columnist for the New York Times, *endorses a proposed soda tax in New York as a way to both raise state revenue and combat obesity.*

As you read, consider the following questions:

1. Why does drinking soda fail to reduce a person's hunger, according to Kristof?

2. Every 10 percent increase in the price of cigarettes reduces sales by what percentage, as noted by the author?

3. How many gallons of soda does the average American drink, according to Kristof?

Nicholas D. Kristof, "Miracle Tax Diet," *New York Times*, December 18, 2008. Reproduced by permission.

When the human body was evolving, almost the only things we drank were breast milk for the first few years and then water, water and more water.

It would obviously have been bad if we had evolved to feel full when water was sloshing about our stomachs because then we wouldn't have eaten our fill the next time we speared a mastodon. Today, the unfortunate result is that if you drink a bottle of 7-Up, you still don't feel full—the body treats the liquid as empty calories, like water—and so you won't eat any less the next time you spear a Big Mac.

That has presented a huge problem in an age of sugary drinks, and some scholars believe they have become a major source of obesity. That's why the new soda tax proposed by Gov. David Paterson of New York is such a breakthrough.

Mr. Paterson suggested the tax—an 18 percent sales tax on soft drinks and other nondiet sugary beverages—to help raise $400 million a year to plug a hole in the state budget. But it's also a landmark effort that, if other states follow, could help make us healthier.

Let's break for a quiz: What was the biggest health care breakthrough in the last 40 years in the United States? Heart bypasses? CAT scans and M.R.I.'s? New cancer treatments?

No, it was the cigarette tax. Every 10 percent price increase on cigarettes reduced sales by about 3 percent over all, and 7 percent among teenagers, according to the 2005 book *Prescription for a Healthy Nation*. Just the 1983 increase in the federal tax on cigarettes saved 40,000 lives per year.

In effect, the most promising cure for lung cancer didn't emerge from a medical research lab but from money-grubbing politicians. Likewise, the best cure for obesity may turn out to be not a pill but a tax.

These days, sugary drinks are to American health roughly what tobacco was a generation ago. A tax would shift some consumers, especially kids, to diet drinks or water.

"Soft drinks are linked to diabetes and obesity in the way that tobacco is to lung cancer," says Barry Popkin, a nutrition specialist at the University of North Carolina and author of the excellent new book, *The World Is Fat*. He warns that the cola industry will spend vast sums fighting the proposed tax.

One of industry's objections is that soft drinks aren't the only problem. That's true, and I'd love to see a "Twinkie tax" as well. But evidence is accumulating that sugary drinks are a major contributor to obesity because of the evolutionary heritage I mentioned at the outset: Except for soups, liquid calories don't register with the body, according to Professor Popkin and other specialists.

If you have a snack, even something unhealthy like potato chips, you'll eat less at your next meal. But have a Coke, and despite all those calories, you'll still eat just as much. Indeed, according to some studies, you'll actually eat more.

"These findings raise the possibility that soft drinks increase hunger, decrease satiety or simply calibrate people to a high level of sweetness that generalizes to preferences in other foods," said a peer-reviewed article [in 2007] in the *American Journal of Public Health*.

The average American consumes about 35 gallons of non-diet soda each year and gets far more added sugar from soda than from desserts.

[U.S. president] Barack Obama has pledged to move toward a system of universal health coverage, and Democrats mostly see health care reform as a matter of providing access to doctors. Access and universal coverage are indeed essential, but there's only so much doctors can do in this environment.

One priority must be a public health campaign to change social behavior. A starting point is to recognize that risky teen behavior these days can involve not just alcohol, drugs or sex but also extra-large Cokes.

One new study estimates that 24 million Americans now have diabetes, more than four times the number in 1980. The total direct and indirect cost to Americans is $218 billion each year—an average of $1,900 per American household. Each year, diabetes contributes to the deaths of more than 200,000 Americans.

Part of the solution must come from reforming agriculture so that we stop subsidizing corn that ends up as high fructose corn syrup inside soft drinks. Unfortunately, Mr. Obama chose Tom Vilsack, the former governor of Iowa who has longstanding ties to agribusiness interests, as agriculture secretary—his weakest selection so far.

The soft-drink industry will throw enormous resources into defeating the proposed New York tax on sugary drinks. We should stand behind Governor Paterson's bold gesture. He is blazing a path that other states should follow.

Losing weight is never easy, but one of the most effective diets would start with a soft drink tax.

| "The food police are closing in on their next target: a soda tax."

Taxing Sugary Drinks Will Not Reduce Obesity

William Saletan

In the following viewpoint, William Saletan opposes the recent movement to add an extra tax to sugary drinks as a way to combat obesity. He contends that this effort is part of an organized strategy to eliminate junk food. Rather than solving the obesity problem, Saletan argues, the soda tax will merely further limit the freedom of Americans to make their own food choices. Saletan is a national correspondent for Slate, *an online magazine.*

As you read, consider the following questions:

1. According to Saletan, to what products do tax proponents compare soda?

2. How does the author respond to the argument that the costs of obesity are paid by Medicare?

3. In Saletan's opinion, why do tax proponents claim the new tax will help children?

The food police are closing in on their next target: a soda tax.

New York City's health commissioner, Thomas Frieden, is leading the way. He's the guy who purged trans fats from the city's restaurants and made them post calorie counts for menu items. Lately he's been pressuring food companies to remove salt from their products.

Now he's going after soda. Writing in the *New England Journal of Medicine* [*NEJM*], Frieden and Kelly Brownell, the director of Yale's Rudd Center for Food Policy and Obesity, propose a penny-per-ounce excise tax on "sugared beverages." That's nearly $3 per case. Why so much? Because this tax, unlike the petty junk-food taxes of yesteryear, is designed to hurt. Its purpose is to discourage you from buying soda, on the grounds that soda, like smoking, is bad for you.

A Political Battle Plan

Persuading Americans to regulate soda the way we regulate cigarettes won't be easy. Isn't soda a kind of food? Isn't food a good thing? And isn't it a matter of personal choice? Doesn't taxation to control people's eating behavior cross a fundamental line of liberty?

In their article, Frieden and Brownell methodically attack these objections. Going well beyond science, they lay out a political battle plan for the war on junk food.

Step 1 is to convince us that soda isn't really food. If you think this can't be done, wake up: Frieden has already done it to trans fats. In the *NEJM* article, he and Brownell spurn the notion that soft drinks are sacred because "people must eat to survive." They tartly observe that "sugared beverages are not necessary for survival."

Step 2 is to associate soda with products we already stigmatize and regulate as harmful. On this point, the authors

Soda Calories Not Uniquely Empty

It's true that, on the whole, fat people drink more soda than skinny people. They also consume more calories overall and exercise less. So soda does help people pack on the pounds. But so does absolutely everything everyone eats. No news story about soda is complete without the scolding phrase "empty calories," yet . . . a food calorie is 4.2 kilojoules of energy, whether it comes from a bottle of orange juice, a latte or an ice-cold Coke. Cola calories are not uniquely "empty." . . . A calorie is a calorie.

Katherine Mangu-Ward,
Washington Post, *September 27, 2009.*

quote [free-market economist] Adam Smith: "Sugar, rum, and tobacco are commodities which are nowhere necessaries of life, which are become objects of almost universal consumption, and which are therefore extremely proper subjects of taxation."

Exaggerated Costs

Step 3 is to persuade you that one person's soda consumption harms others, thereby transcending personal liberty. The authors write:

> The contribution of unhealthful diets to health care costs is already high and is increasing—an estimated $79 billion is spent annually for overweight and obesity alone—and approximately half of these costs are paid by Medicare and Medicaid, at taxpayers' expense. Diet-related diseases also cost society in terms of decreased work productivity, in-

creased absenteeism, poorer school performance, and reduced fitness on the part of military recruits, among other
negative effects.

The Medicare argument is dubious, since, as my colleague
Daniel Engber points out, fat people die younger and thereby
save the program years of coverage. But the really cheeky
pitch is the one about military recruits. Apparently, Coke is
now a menace to national security.

Step 4 is to target kids, because our urge to protect them
makes us more amenable to paternalism. "Sugared beverages
are marketed extensively to children and adolescents" and
"now account for 10 to 15% of the calories consumed by children and adolescents," Frieden and Brownell observe. In fact,
soda makers "exploit the cognitive vulnerabilities of young
children, who often cannot distinguish a television program
from an advertisement." New York Mayor Michael Bloomberg
echoes this plea: "We have to do something to help our children."

Step 5 is to tempt policymakers with cash flow. "A third
consideration is revenue generation," the authors note. "A
penny-per-ounce excise tax would raise an estimated $1.2 bil-
lion in New York State alone."

Step 6 is to persuade voters that the tax is for their health,
not for cash flow. Frieden and Brownell note the political importance of this message: "[A] poll of New York residents
found that 52% supported a 'soda tax,' but the number rose to
72% when respondents were told that the revenue would be
used for obesity prevention."

Behavior Modification Through Taxation

Three years ago [in 2006], I thought the movement to legis-
late against junk food was politically futile. But that was before the successful assaults on trans fats, calorie counts, and
opening fast-food restaurants. Those victories, apparently,
were just the appetizers. The next course is behavior modifica-
tion through taxation. And this article is the recipe.

Periodical Bibliography

The following articles have been selected to supplement the diverse views presented in this chapter.

Kayce T. Ataiyero   "Diet Aids May Slim Only Your Wallet," *Chicago Tribune*, December 30, 2008.

Kelly D. Brownell et al.   "The Public Health and Economic Benefits of Taxing Sugar-Sweetened Beverages," *New England Journal of Medicine*, October 15, 2009.

John Cloud   "Why Exercise Won't Make You Thin," *Time*, August 9, 2009.

Harold Goldstein and Eric Schlosser   "Putting Health on the Menu," *Los Angeles Times*, August 5, 2009.

Derrick Z. Jackson   "Soda Tax: It's the Real Thing," *Boston Globe*, September 19, 2009.

Jeff Jacoby   "Want a Warning Label with Those Fries?" *Boston Globe*, January 11, 2009.

Jim Kling   "An Overweight Man Learns He Can't Hide Behind His Mom's Genes," *Washington Post*, February 24, 2009.

Katherine Mangu-Ward   "Five Myths About Sin Taxes on Soda," *Washington Post*, September 27, 2009.

Henry Miller   "Foolish Food Fads," *Washington Times*, January 3, 2008.

Shari Roan   "Gastric Bypass Before Babies?" *Los Angeles Times*, September 7, 2009.

Jacob Sullum   "Are You *Sure* You Want Fries with That?" *Reason*, August 20, 2008.

For Further Discussion

Chapter 1

1. Sarah Baldauf describes several health problems that are believed to be caused or made worse by obesity. Paul Campos discusses research purporting to show that being overweight does not increase one's risk of death. After reading both viewpoints, do you think being obese is unhealthy? Support your answer with references to the viewpoints.

2. The viewpoint by the Centers for Disease Control and Prevention states that more schools are instituting programs to improve the nutrition and increase the physical activity of students. Does your school have such programs? Is your school doing enough to reduce obesity among students? Defend your answer with examples.

Chapter 2

1. Patti Miller argues that food advertising contributes to obesity among young people. Do you think you are influenced by advertising to eat or drink unhealthy products, such as fast foods and soft drinks? Explain why or why not. Identify one ad for snacks, sodas, or fast food and explain why it is or is not persuasive.

Chapter 3

1. Jeremy Brown contends that doctors must do a better job of addressing obesity in their patients. Victoria McEvoy argues that solving the obesity problem will require the involvement of all of society. After reading these viewpoints, do you think doctors can do much to reduce obesity? Why or why not?

2. After reading all the viewpoints in this chapter, who do you think must take responsibility for obesity—the government, doctors, schools, parents, or obese individuals? Support your answer with references to the viewpoints.

Chapter 4

1. Anne Moore uses her personal experience to argue that it is possible to lose weight by means of diet and exercise. Judy Foreman cites scientific research to support her position that it is nearly impossible to lose a significant amount of weight through diet and exercise. Which type of argument—personal testimony or scientific citations—do you find more persuasive, and why?

2. Cassie Pisano describes her positive experience with gastric bypass surgery. Sabrina Rubin Erdely presents several cases in which patients experienced severe side effects from the procedure. After reading these two viewpoints, do you think gastric bypass surgery is safe or dangerous? What additional information do you need in order to make a final decision? Explain your answer.

3. Nicholas D. Kristof argues that increasing taxes on sugary drinks will help prevent obesity. William Saletan opposes this policy change. Based on these viewpoints, do you think raising taxes will prevent young people from drinking soda and other sugary beverages? Why or why not?

Organizations to Contact

The editors have compiled the following list of organizations concerned with the issues debated in this book. The descriptions are derived from materials provided by the organizations. All have publications or information available for interested readers. The list was compiled on the date of publication of the present volume; the information provided here may change. Be aware that many organizations take several weeks or longer to respond to inquiries, so allow as much time as possible.

American Academy of Pediatrics (AAP)
141 Northwest Point Blvd., Elk Grove Village, IL   60007
(847) 434-4000 • fax: (847) 434-8000
e-mail: commun@aap.org
Web site: www.aap.org

The American Academy of Pediatrics is a membership organization of physicians dedicated to the health and well-being of children. Its Web site includes an overweight and obesity section that provides documents and audio files on the causes and treatments of childhood obesity for both parents and professionals.

American Heart Association (AHA)
National Center, 7272 Greenville Ave., Dallas, TX   75231
(800) 242-8721
Web site: www.americanheart.org

The American Heart Association is a national voluntary health agency that promotes cardiovascular health. Its Web site provides information on overweight conditions and obesity and their relation to various diseases such as stroke and cardiac arrest. The AHA publishes brochures such as "Managing Your Weight" and "Just Move!" as well as facts sheets, including "How Can I Cook Healthfully?" and "How Do I Read Food Labels?"

American Society for Metabolic and Bariatric Surgery (ASMBS)

100 SW Seventy-fifth St., Suite 201, Gainesville, FL   32607
(352) 331-4900 • fax: (352) 331-4975
e-mail: info@asmbs.org
Web site: www.asmbs.org

The ASMBS works to advance bariatric surgery through investigation, idea exchange, and educational programs. Its Web site supplies information for patients and health-care professionals about bariatric surgery and the society's meetings and classes.

Center for Science in the Public Interest (CSPI)

1875 Connecticut Ave. NW, Suite 300, Washington, DC   20009
(202) 332-9110 • fax: (202) 265-4954
e-mail: cspi@cspinet.org
Web site: www.cspinet.org

The Center for Science in the Public Interest is a nonprofit organization that advocates policies that promote nutrition and health, food safety, and sound science. It frequently reports on the excessive fat, sugar, and salt content of foods Americans consume. Its Web site offers numerous fact sheets and articles on obesity and ways to prevent it, including a tax on sugary drinks. CSPI also publishes the health newsletter *Nutrition Action Healthletter*.

Centers for Disease Control and Prevention (CDC)

1600 Clifton Rd., Atlanta, GA   30333
(800) 232-4636
e-mail: cdcinfo@cdc.gov
Web site: www.cdc.gov

The CDC, part of the U.S. Department of Health and Human Services, is the department of the federal government responsible for monitoring and responding to the nation's health problems. Its Web site presents information and statistics on obesity in the United States and offers recommendations for communities and schools to reduce obesity among the population.

International Association for the Study of Obesity (IASO)
28 Portland Place, London   W1B 1LY
  United Kingdom
44-20-7467-9610
e-mail: enquiries@iaso.org
Web site: www.iaso.org

The International Association for the Study of Obesity is a nonprofit umbrella organization of national obesity associations. It includes fifty-two member national obesity organizations representing fifty-six countries. The IASO publishes three journals, and its working groups on childhood obesity, obesity prevention, and other specialties present their latest findings on the organization's Web site.

National Association to Advance Fat Acceptance (NAAFA)
PO Box 22510, Oakland, CA   94609
(916) 558-6880
Web site: www.naafaonline.com/dev2

The National Association to Advance Fat Acceptance is a civil rights organization working to improve the lives of people whom society labels overweight or obese. It works to end discrimination against fat people in the workplace, education system, and health-care system. The NAAFA's Web site offers links to resources on anti–fat discrimination legislation and on staying healthy at any size.

National Institutes of Health (NIH)
9000 Rockville Pike, Bethesda, MD   20892
(301) 496-4000
e-mail: nihinfo@od.nih.gov
Web site: www.nih.gov

The NIH, part of the U.S. Department of Health and Human Services, is the main federal agency responsible for medical research. It consists of twenty-seven institutes and centers that conduct research in specialized areas. Several of these institutes, including the National Institute of Diabetes and Digestive and Kidney Diseases and the National Heart, Lung, and Blood Institute, offer fact sheets, reports, and other resources related to obesity.

Obesity Action Coalition

4511 N. Himes Ave., Suite 250, Tampa, FL 33614
(800) 717-3117 • fax: (813) 873-7838
e-mail: info@obesityaction.org
Web site: www.obesityaction.org

The Obesity Action Coalition is a nonprofit advocacy organization that aims to empower and educate those affected by obesity. It offers free resources on obesity, morbid obesity, and childhood obesity, in addition to consequences and treatments of these conditions. The coalition's publications include fact sheets, brochures, and the magazine *Your Weight Matters.*

Obesity in America

8401 Connecticut Ave., Suite 900, Chevy Chase, MD 20815
(301) 941-0200
e-mail: media@endo-society.org
Web site: www.obesityinamerica.org

Obesity in America was created by the Endocrine Society and the Hormone Foundation to serve as a clearinghouse for information on the scientific trends and advancements in the battle against obesity. Its Web site offers statistics and news reports on the latest research into the causes and treatments of obesity.

Obesity Society

8630 Fenton St., Suite 814, Silver Spring, MD 20910
(301) 563-6526 • fax: (301) 563-6595
Web site: www.obesity.org

The Obesity Society is a scientific research organization that studies the causes, treatments, and prevention of obesity and informs the public of new developments. Its Web site provides fact sheets and statistics on obesity. The society holds an annual conference and publishes a newsletter and the journal *Obesity.*

Reason Foundation

3415 S. Sepulveda Blvd., Suite 400, Los Angeles, CA 90034
(310) 391-2245 • fax: (310) 391-4395
Web site: www.reason.org

The Reason Foundation is a nonprofit, libertarian research organization. It advocates limited government regulation of people's personal lives. Therefore, the foundation opposes legislation to impose added taxes on sugary drinks or require fast food restaurants to post their meals' calorie counts on their menu boards.

Shape Up America!

Web site: www.shapeup.org

Shape Up America! is a nonprofit organization dedicated to public education regarding the harms of obesity and how to prevent them through increased exercise and healthy eating. Its Web site provides detailed advice for individuals, parents, and educators on achieving a healthy body weight. It also publishes a monthly newsletter.

U.S. Department of Health and Human Services

200 Independence Ave. SW, Washington, DC 20201
(877) 696-6775
Web site: www.hhs.gov

The U.S. Department of Health and Human Services is the principal division of the federal government responsible for protecting the nation's health. Its Web site provides fact sheets and brochures on obesity as well as on how to prevent it by means of healthy diet and exercise. Titles include "Help Your Child Stay at a Healthy Weight" and "Learn About Overweight and Obesity."

World Health Organization (WHO)

Avenue Appia 20, Geneva 27 1211
  Switzerland
41-22-791-21-11 • fax: 41-22-791-31-11

e-mail: info@who.int
Web site: www.who.int

The World Health Organization is the division of the United Nations responsible for monitoring global health and responding to international health crises. Its Global Strategy on Diet, Physical Activity and Health offers information on obesity among both children and adults worldwide as well as recommendations for individuals, communities, and governments on how to solve the problem.

Bibliography of Books

America's Trust for Health — *F as in Fat: How Obesity Policies Are Failing America.* Washington, DC: America's Trust for Health, 2009.

Eric J. Bailey — *Food Choice and Obesity in Black America: Creating a New Cultural Diet.* Westport, CT: Praeger, 2006.

Kelly D. Brownell — *Food Fight: The Inside Story of the Food Industry, America's Obesity Crisis, and What We Can Do About It.* New York: McGraw-Hill, 2004.

Ian W. Campbell — *Obesity: Your Questions Answered.* New York: Churchill Livingstone, 2005.

Paul F. Campos — *The Obesity Myth: Why America's Obsession with Weight Is Hazardous to Your Health.* New York: Gotham, 2004.

Hank Cardello, with Doug Garr — *Stuffed: An Insider's Look at Who's (Really) Making America Fat.* New York: Ecco, 2009.

Greg Crister — *Fat Land: How Americans Became the Fattest People in the World.* Boston: Houghton Mifflin, 2004.

Garth Davis — *The Expert's Guide to Weight-Loss Surgery: Is It Right for Me? What Happens During Surgery? How Do I Keep the Weight Off?* New York: Hudson Street, 2009.

Nancy Deville   *Death by Supermarket: The Fattening, Dumbing Down, and Poisoning of America.* Fort Lee, NJ: Barricade, 2007.

Kathi A. Earles   *Scale Back: Why Childhood Obesity Is*
and Sandra E.   *Not Just About Weight.* Chicago:
Moore   Hilton, 2008.

Eric A. Finkelstein *The Fattening of America: How the*
and Laurie   *Economy Makes Us Fat, If It Matters,*
Zuckerman   *and What to Do About It.* Hoboken, NJ: Wiley, 2008.

Sander L. Gilman   *Fat: A Cultural History of Obesity.* Cambridge, UK: Polity, 2008.

Rhonda L.   *A Guide to Weight Loss Surgery:*
Hamilton   *Professional and Personal Views.* Westport, CT: Praeger, 2008.

Richard J.   *The Sugar Fix: The High-Fructose*
Johnson   *Fallout That Is Making You Fat and Sick.* Emmaus, PA: Rodale, 2008.

David A. Kessler   *The End of Overeating: Taking Control of the Insatiable American Appetite.* Emmaus, PA: Rodale, 2009.

Elaine D. Kolish   *Changing the Landscape of Food and*
and C. Lee Peeler   *Beverage Advertising: The Children's Food and Beverage Advertising Initiative in Action.* Arlington, VA: Council of Better Business Bureaus, 2008.

Don Kulick   *Fat: The Anthropology of an Obsession.* New York: Jeremy P. Tarcher/Penguin, 2005.

James Levine   *Move a Little, Lose a Lot: New NEAT Science Reveals How to Be Thinner, Happier, and Smarter.* New York: Crown, 2009.

J. Michael   *Food Marketing to Children and Youth: Threat or Opportunity?* Washington, DC: National Academies, 2006.
McGinnis,
Jennifer Appleton
Gootman, and
Vivica I. Kraak,
eds.

Susan Okie   *Fed Up! Winning the War Against Childhood Obesity.* Washington, DC: Joseph Henry, 2005.

Eric J. Oliver   *Fat Politics: The Real Story Behind America's Obesity Epidemic.* New York: Oxford University Press, 2006.

Lynn Parker,   *Local Government Action to Prevent Childhood Obesity.* Washington, DC: National Academies, 2009.
Annina Catherine
Burns, and
Eduardo Sanchez,
eds.

Barry Popkin   *The World Is Fat: The Fads, Trends, Policies, and Products That Are Fattening the Human Race.* New York: Penguin, 2009.

Michael L. Power   *The Evolution of Obesity.* Baltimore: Johns Hopkins University Press, 2009.

Alexander G.   *Obesity: Why Are Men Getting Pregnant?* Laguna Beach, CA: Basic Health, 2006.
Schauss

Patricia K. Smith   *Obesity Among Poor Americans: Is Public Assistance the Problem?* Nashville: Vanderbilt University Press, 2009.

Linda Smolak   *Body Image, Eating Disorders, and Obesity in Youth: Assessment, Prevention, and Treatment.* 2nd ed. Washington, DC: American Psychological Association, 2009.

Lisa Tartamella   *Generation Extra Large: Rescuing Our Children from an Epidemic of Obesity.* New York: Basic Books, 2004.

Index